Why Isn't God Giving Cash Prizes?

Lorraine Peterson

BETHANY HOUSE PUBLISHERS
MINNEAPOLIS, MINNESOTA 55438
A Division of Bethany Fellowship, Inc.

About the Author

LORRAINE PETERSON was born in Red Wing, Minnesota, grew up on a farm near Ellsworth, Wisconsin, and now is a teacher at the American School in Guadalajara, Mexico. She received her B.A. (in history) from North Park College in Chicago, and has taken summer courses from the University of Minnesota and the University of Mexico in Mexico City.

Lorraine has taught high school and junior high. She has been an advisor to nondenominational Christian clubs in Minneapolis public schools and has taught teenage Bible studies. She has written two best-selling devotional books for teens: *If God Loves Me, Why Can't I Get My Locker Open?* and *Falling Off Cloud Nine and Other High Places.*

The Scripture quotations in this publication are from the Revised Standard Version of the Bible, copyrighted 1946, 1952 © 1971, 1973 by the Division of Christian Education of the National Council of the Churches of Christ in the U.S.A., and used by permission.

Illustrations by LeRoy Dugan.

Published by Bethany House Publishers
A Division of Bethany Fellowship, Inc.
6820 Auto Club Road, Minneapolis, Minnesota 55438

Printed in the United States of America

Peterson, Lorraine.
   Why isn't God giving cash prizes?

   (Devotionals for teens; #3)
   Summary: A thirteen-week program of devotional study exploring the existence and nature of God and other theological questions.
   1. Youth—Prayer-books and devotions—English.
[1. Prayer books and devotions.   2. Theology]
I. Title.   II. Series.
BV4850.P465   1982   230   82-17866
ISBN 0-87123-626-5 (pbk.)

Preface

Why build a devotional book around apologetics and doctrine? After all, shouldn't the thought for the day be only some beautiful words which give a feeling of inspiration? Shouldn't reasons and explanations for our beliefs be left in bound volumes on library shelves for intellectuals to read?

Well, Clark H. Pinnock, an intellectual, says, "Apologetics is related to *worship* too. It is always a joyous discovery to see afresh the adequacy and firmness of God's truth. Christian worship . . . arises in the soul fixed in adoration and contemplation of God's truth." I agree with him.

I've chosen this format for another reason as well. I know that if young people do not first learn the truth, they will fall prey to false beliefs. They will be easily deceived.

I once sat in an airplane next to a nice-looking young girl who had joined a notorious modern cult. As she explained what she believed, I commented, "You wouldn't believe that if you had ever read and studied the Bible *before* you joined the group."

She admitted that although she had a church background, she had never studied the Bible on her own. The experience of this girl and other young people I have known has convinced me that this book is needed.

The book, *Why Isn't God Giving Cash Prizes?* gives scriptural answers to questions which non-Christians often ask. It is geared for teenagers and can be understood without a lot of educational background. This sets it apart from the many excellent books which have been written in this field.

On the other hand, discussing complicated theological questions in an easy-to-understand manner is hard to do and I do not claim infallibility. Those who teach from this book may want to add or delete. Although I am praying that God will use this book in the lives of teenagers, we must all be aware that no book can lead us into all truth. Only the Holy Spirit can do that.

I owe much to those whose research and teaching have provided the information needed to write this book. My pastor, the Rev. Ernest O'Neill of Campus Church, has given some excellent sermons on apologetics. I've also learned much from the courses I've taken at the Christian Corps Training School sponsored by Campus

Church. The research of Josh McDowell, John R.W. Stott and Richard Wolff has contributed to this book. Those who have read Francis Schaeffer will recognize his influence on my writing. Walter Martin's book, *The Kingdom of the Cults,* and the publications of the Spiritual Counterfeits Project proved to be invaluable resources.

Special thanks go to: Michael O'Connor for proofreading my manuscript and offering many valuable suggestions; the students I've taught; the teens in my Bible study groups who have shared their world with me; my father who made copies of my manuscript and helped me in many ways; my sister, my brother-in-law, and my nieces and nephews, Beth, Brett, Kaari and Kirk, who constantly supported and encouraged me.

Table of Contents

How to Use This Book

To teenagers for daily devotions: In order to get the most out of these lessons, keep a notebook and *write down* the answers. The lazy part of you is saying, "I don't want to—it's too much work." However, education research supports the idea that you remember things you write down longer than things you only think about. God's Word is very important—important enough to get your best effort.

To youth workers for Sunday school or Bible study material: Leaders should assign the daily readings for the week. Ask students to write out the answers to the questions along with any new questions which they would like to discuss with the group. The leader can pick out the most important questions and ask members to contribute their findings. If it is not practical for your group to prepare in advance, it would be better to spend at least two weeks on each topic, read the material in class, and cover the questions as you go along. The teacher will want to add questions and thoughts which are relevant to the particular group being taught.

Week One

GOD, ARE YOU THERE?

In the Beginning God

Does your biology book claim that life just happened without any Creator? Some biology texts, though they do not give *God* the credit for making the world, are honest enough not to make up their own creation story. For example, one such book says, "The question of how life originated remains open to investigation."[1] But if your science teacher explains in detail how energy over zillions of years formed toadstools, horned owls, and Mrs. Jones, don't decide to resign from the human race or throw out the Bible. Just do some thinking.

Where did the universe with oak trees, chattering squirrels, inquisitive three-year-olds, and solar systems come from? There are only three possibilities: 1) It came from nothing; 2) It came from something non-living and impersonal; 3) It began with a Personal Being. Since no one believes it came from absolutely nothing, we won't bother to discuss that possibility.

If everything began with something impersonal, such as mass, energy, or motion, why do people have individual personalities, consciences and curiosity? Did simple energy form into individual beings with intelligence, emotions and a hunger to know God? The formula for this theory seems to be: *the impersonal + chance + time.* Yet, most people would not consider throwing the parts of a watch into an electric washing machine, expecting the energy to produce a watch—even if the machine could run for a billion years. It seems even less likely that energy could generate the *parts* of a watch no matter how many billion years were involved. And we haven't even discussed how *living* things originated.

Francis Schaeffer writes, "No one has ever thought of a way of deriving personality from a nonpersonal source."[2] How could man with his feelings of hope, significance, purpose, love, guilt, and his ability to communicate verbally have been created by something which did not have personality?

However, if a Personal Being created everything, there is an explanation for man's questioning mind, his creative genius, and his capacity for caring about others. Also, if a personal God created *you*, there is a reason for your existence. You weren't a chance occurrence. God created you to be something special. When you feel blah and worthless, turn to your Creator and thank Him for creating you to be unique, to think special thoughts, and to help others in a way that no one else can. Then ask Him what important thing He wants you to do each day.

"By the word of the Lord the heavens were made, and all their host by the breath of his mouth" (Ps. 33:6).

" 'Thou didst clothe me with skin and flesh, and knit me together with bones and sinews' " (Job 10:11).

"Thy hands have made and fashioned me; give me understanding that I may learn thy commandments" (Ps. 119:73).

1. God took special time and care in creating you. How can this fact improve your self-concept?
2. Why is it harmful for people to believe that they are products of chance?
3. Which of your unique characteristics will you thank God for today?

Do You Worship Purple Protoplasm?

"The God I worship is a God of love who wouldn't send anyone to hell." "I don't believe in a God who won't give me freedom." "Belief in a Father, Son and Holy Spirit is illogical."

What do we do with statements like that? Maybe we should consider one fundamental question: *Did you create God or did He create you?*

I could never get by with saying "In my opinion, George Washington never was involved in any war because only a peaceful man should be the 'father of this country.' " People would be equally unimpressed with my stating, "The concept of a round earth is ridiculous, I'm convinced that the earth is flat."

Either God exists or He doesn't. In either case, a god you made up in your mind is less important than you are because the creator is always above his or her creation. A god you (or anyone else) made up could be a wooden idol, purple protoplasm, an all-powerful Santa Claus, or a hideous Hitler; but that wouldn't make a real person come into being.

God is God and He defines himself. There is only one person in history who claimed that God was His father and that He knew exactly what God is like. Jesus of Nazareth claimed to be the Son of the Creator of the universe. His moral life, His miracles, and His resurrection from death proved that He knew what He was talking about. The Gospels record what He had to say about God.

God also reveals or shows himself to people. Those who give up their imagined god and diligently seek to know God will find Him. Isaiah 65:1 says, "I was ready to be sought by those who did not ask for me; I was ready to be found by those who did not seek me." We need "to humble ourselves, to listen and learn of Him, and to let Him teach us what he is like and how we should think of Him."[3]

It is too easy even for Christians who believe every word the Bible uses to describe God to become guilty of making up their own God. They construct a God who doesn't attend football games, a God who plugs His ears when teens talk back to their parents, or a God who can't empower young people to stand against peer pressure. They don't turn to the Bible to find out what God's really like. They rely on things they have heard or on their own assumptions. Are you willing to let God be God? Or are you creating your own purple protoplasm deity?

" 'Behold, I am the Lord, the God of all flesh; is anything too hard for me?' " (Jer. 32:27).

"The eyes of the Lord are in every place, keeping watch on the evil and the good" (Prov. 15:3).

"Thus says God, the Lord, who created the heavens and stretched them out, who spread forth the earth and what comes from it, . . . 'I am the Lord, that is my name; my glory I give to no other, nor my praise to graven images' " (Isa. 42:5, 8).

1. Are you living as though you have a problem too great for God to solve? Discuss this with God and ask Him to show you His power.
2. Do you act as if God doesn't see your reaction when you strike out in the bottom of the ninth or receive a D in physics?
3. Is there anything or anyone whom you admire more than God? Are you willing to face this honestly or are you just hoping God won't notice? What does God have to say about sharing His glory with another?

The Loudspeaker in the Sky

Imagine coming home from school and finding a black Trans-Am Firebird in your driveway. As you look closer you see an envelope on the windshield with your name on it. In the envelope is a set

of keys and a little card which says, "A gift for you!" Wouldn't your first question be, "Who put this here?"

Honestly, what would your reply be to your little sister if she declares, "There must have been an explosion"?

Is it really possible for thinking people to see a baby's smile, the dew on a rosebud, or a snow-covered mountain without asking, "Who made all this?" Does a "big bang theory" really seem like an adequate explanation?

Okay, so you can't put God in a test tube and "prove" Him by a repeatable experiment, but then you can't prove Napoleon or Abraham Lincoln by that method either. Just because we can't produce reruns of the creation of the universe, the fall of Rome, or the American Revolution does not mean that these events did not take place. Laboratory experiments were not meant to prove God or love or justice or anger. But even if you haven't seen a yard of love or a quart of justice, that's not proof that they don't exist.

Somebody very intelligent must have created this universe,

which is so predictable that every time one part of hydrogen is combined with two parts of oxygen water is produced. Actually, scientific experiments are possible *only* because of this predictability. Every detail of creation is perfect. The earth is exactly the right distance from the sun so that we neither burn up nor freeze to death. There is just the right amount of water in the oceans to act as the world's thermostat.

The fact that all the things that exist advertise a Creator God is called "natural revelation." The fluffy clouds and sparkling stars are really God's loudspeaker in the sky saying to anyone who will listen, "Look at all the neat things I've made." According to the space museum in Washington, D.C., there are over one hundred billion galaxies in our universe. It seems obvious that all this has been made by Someone very powerful. If your science teacher or your textbook chooses to ignore that loudspeaker in the sky, don't panic. The God who created the Great Lakes and the Rocky Mountains is able to defend himself. You can relax and trust Him.

"The heavens are telling the glory of God; and the firmament proclaims his handiwork. Day to day pours forth speech, and night to night declares knowledge. There is no speech, nor are there words; their voice is not heard; yet their voice goes out through all the earth, and their words to the end of the world" (Ps. 19:1-4).

"Who has measured the waters in the hollow of his hand and marked off the heavens with a span, enclosed the dust of the earth in a measure and weighed the mountains in scales and the hills in a balance?" (Isa. 40:12).

1. In what ways do you think that the sky advertises the glory of God?
2. Why do the mountains, which seem so big to us, seem so small to God?
3. Do you live as though the Creator of the universe might be able to help you study for the algebra test or show you how to discuss a problem with your mother?

Isosceles Triangles and the God Who Is There

Does your daily routine seem like a drag? Are you thinking, "What difference does it make if an isosceles triangle has equal sides or not? Why do I need to know what a subordinate clause is, or remember what happened in 1776?" What's more, you may be wondering why you should think of the future at all. Some insane dictator might blow us off the face of the earth tomorrow, anyway. Does it really matter if you do your assignments, hold down a job, or pay your bills? If there is nothing but death and oblivion to look forward to, is it important how you live your life?

If there is not a personal, knowable God, the particulars of life don't have any significance. If your beginning was an accident of energy and your end is complete nothingness, the details of your life have no meaning. If there is no God, it doesn't matter if you're good or bad, neat or messy, studious or lazy. Even the argument that you have an obligation to other people or to society seems weak if your best friend lets you down.

People who don't believe in God believe, deep down, that life is a farce. So they try to create some meaning. The things-will-get-better-tomorrow philosophy or the live-for-all-the-fun-you-can-get routine are attempts to find purpose in life. Some people just take a "leap of faith" and try to believe that everything is good and beautiful, even if that is contrary to reason.

But you can know the Creator of the universe *personally* through faith in Jesus Christ. When there is no one else to talk to, God is there to notice your success and to share your heartache. You can make your bed and keep your room clean in order to glorify God. You can find meaning in ordinary things, because doing your best is a way of worshiping God.

The Bible teaches that there is life after death and that evil will be punished and good will be rewarded. But right now He has a great purpose for you—to spread His peace and His order throughout the universe. Your smile, your encouraging words, and your willingness to obey Jesus are part of God's plan for the universe. The real God does make a difference in how you approach isosceles triangles.

"Let the words of my mouth and the meditation of my heart be acceptable in thy sight, O Lord, my rock and my redeemer" (Ps. 19:14).

"So, whether you eat or drink, or whatever you do, do all to the glory of God" (1 Cor. 10:31).

"And whatever you do, in word or deed, do everything in the name of the Lord Jesus, giving thanks to God the Father through him" (Col. 3:17).

1. Do you run some areas of your life as though God didn't exist?

2. How about doing the math assignment and cleaning your room with God in mind?
3. How can a strong belief in God's purpose for you prevent discouragement?
4. How would you respond to the person who says, "It doesn't make any difference whether or not I believe in God"?

What Does God Look Like?

When you think of God, what picture comes to your mind? Do you think of a kind-looking old gentleman in a rocking chair on some cloud? A "no you can't" computer? An enlarged replica of your father when he's angry? The Bible says God is none of these. Jesus taught that "God is *spirit*, and those who worship him must worship in spirit and truth" (John 4:24).

Although God the Father does not have a physical body, Christ at times took on a physical body to appear during Old Testament times. For example, when three men were thrown into a flaming furnace for refusing to worship an idol, everyone plainly saw a fourth whom King Nebuchadnezzar described as "like a son of the gods" (Dan. 3:25). Christ had come to save them.

The Jesus who was born in Bethlehem had a physical body, but He let people worship Him as God. After He rose from the dead, He continued to have a body. Zechariah predicts that when Jesus comes back again, His *feet* will touch the Mount of Olives and people will "*look* on him whom they have pierced" (Zech. 14:4; 12:10).

John 1:18 sums it up: "No one has ever seen God; the only Son, who is in the bosom of the Father, he has made him known." We can't see God the Father. Therefore, Jesus was sent so man could know what God is like. His physical appearance (and it varied throughout the Old Testament) was never important. It was His *character* that everybody noticed. "The Word became flesh [Jesus] and dwelt among us, full of grace and truth" (John 1:14).

Jesus explained that, although God is spirit, He himself has a physical body: " 'See my hands and my feet, that it is myself; handle me, and see; for a spirit has not flesh and bones as you see that I have' " (Luke 24:39).

That is why Isaiah could say, "I saw the Lord sitting upon a throne high and lifted up" (Isa. 6:1). Isaiah had a vision of *Jesus*; he did not see God the Father. Jesus taught that He was the only person who had ever seen the Father (John 6:46). But many have seen God the Son—Jesus.

Perhaps you feel gypped because the disciples got to see Jesus personally, and you can't. Just remember what Jesus said to Thomas: "Have you believed because you have seen me? Blessed are those who have *not seen* and yet believe" (John 20:29).

"Philip said to him, 'Lord, show us the Father, and we shall be satisfied.' Jesus said to him, 'Have I been with you so long, and yet you do not know me, Philip? He who has seen me has seen the Father; how can you say, "Show us the Father"? Do you not believe that I am in the Father and the Father in me?' " (John 14:8-10).

1. Though we cannot know what God *looks* like, what *can* we know about Him?
2. Why do you think it's more "blessed" to believe in God without having seen Jesus?
3. If someone told you that God the Father looked like a human being, what would you tell that person?

What Is God's Name?

Several names for God are used in the Bible to describe His wonderful characteristics. *El* or *Elohim* (*Theos* or mighty God in the Greek of the New Testament) is a name for God which stresses that He is strong and preeminent. *Elyon* or Most High shows that He is to be the object of our worship. *Adonai,* another Hebrew name for God, which is usually translated Lord in our English Bibles, shows that He is the owner and ruler of mankind. *Shaddai* or *El Shaddai* recognizes that God is almighty.

Jehovah or Yahweh is the name by which God reveals himself as the God of grace—the God who cares about us personally and gives us the forgiveness, love, and favor that we do not deserve. In Exodus, chapter three, after God tells Moses to lead His people out of Egypt, Moses asked God, "What is your name?" God said to Moses, " 'I am who I am.' " This name comes from the Hebrew verb to be, and "I am" shows how faithful God is, has been, and will be, in keeping His promise.

Since the Hebrew written language has no vowels and they are only inserted by the oral reader, this name for God is written YHWH or JHVH in the Hebrew language. Because God especially revealed this name to Moses, it was considered the most holy name for God. One of the Ten Commandments tells us not to use the name of God carelessly. About 300 B.C. the Jews decided never to say YHWH out loud in order to keep from breaking this command-ment. Interestingly enough, the actual pronunciation has been for-gotten, so *no one* knows what the vowels are. Putting the name into English presents another problem since our consonant sounds are not the same as the Hebrew ones. Yahweh has been used, but dif-ferent vowels could be substituted. Jehovah was the first attempt to translate it into English. However, Johevah or Jihivih could have been used instead. (The Moabite Stone, an inscription written by the neighbors of Israel about 800 B.C., does refer to the God of Israel as Yahweh.[4])

The name Jehovah or Yahweh is not used in the oldest Greek manuscripts of the New Testament. "Kurios . . . the word for Lord in Greek is a name that is applied not only to God but also to Christ. It takes the place of both Adonai and Jehovah."[5] Walter Martin, an authority in the field, says this: "It can be shown from literally thousands of copies of the Greek New Testament that not once does the tetragrammaton [YHWH] appear."[6]

Jehovah or Yahweh in the Old Testament is described in many ways that show us all that our God can be for us! *Jehovah-ropheka* (Jehovah that healeth thee); *Jehovah-roi* (Jehovah my shepherd); *Jehovah-Jireh* (Jehovah will provide); and *Jehovah-shalom* (Jeho-vah is peace) are some of these.

"Jesus said to them, 'Truly, truly I say to you, before Abraham was, I am.' So they took up stones to throw at him; but Jesus hid himself, and went out of the temple" (John 8:58, 59).

"Again the high priest asked him, 'Are you the Christ, the Son of the Blessed?' And Jesus said, 'I am; and you will see the Son of man seated at the right hand of Power, and coming with the clouds of heaven.' And the high priest tore his garments, and said, 'Why do we still need witnesses? You have heard his blasphemy [speaking lightly or carelessly of God, a crime punishable by death under He-brew law]. What is your decision?' " (Mark 14:61-64).

1. Why do you think the Jewish leaders were so upset when Jesus used the words "I am" to describe himself?
2. Why is it significant that Jesus said, "Before Abraham was *I am*," instead of just explaining that He existed before Abraham?
3. As you consider the things you face this week, which names of God do you need to think about and depend on?

God Doesn't Need an Afternoon Nap

God has personality. He has intelligence, will, and the ability to reason and to make decisions. He creates things—like the universe, for example! Scripture tells us that God remembers, He knows, He hears, He sees, He speaks, and He will judge us. In the Bible He is represented as a personal God with whom we can talk, a God who helps us with our problems and fills our hearts with joy and victory.

God has given personality to each of us as well. This is the sense in which we are created in the image of God. Our conscience, concern about life after death, and ability to reason and use language are some of the things that separate us from animals, plants and machines. However, even though God is personal, it is easy to oversimplify this into thinking of God as a being exactly like ourselves who changes His socks, needs an afternoon nap, and takes vitamin pills.

God is not only personal; He is infinite—boundless, limitless and perfect. He is not restricted by any body, for He is Spirit. God has always existed and always will. He needs the help of nobody. In these ways God is set apart from His entire creation. And in the sense of being finite, of having many limitations, and of facing certain death, man is somewhat like all animals and plants.

Although God is so great that we'll never adequately understand Him, remember that He is personal and therefore concerned about every detail of *your* life—your date on Friday night, your getting that job at MacDonald's and your finding the history report you just lost. Because God is infinite, there is nothing He cannot do. Give Him your toughest problems and let Him solve them. Remember that He is with you always, understanding you when no one else seems to care. He'll never take a nap and leave you to fend for yourself.

"For he has said, 'I will never fail you nor forsake you'" (Heb. 13:5).

"For thus says the most high and lofty One who inhabits eternity, whose name is Holy: 'I dwell in the high and holy place, and also with him who is of a contrite and humble spirit, to revive the spirit of the humble, and to revive the heart of the contrite [acknowledging guilt]'" (Isa. 57:15).

" 'Can a man hide himself in secret places so that I cannot see him? says the Lord. Do I not fill the heavens and the earth? says the Lord" (Jer. 23:24).

" 'Who is like thee, O Lord, among the gods? Who is like thee, majestic in holiness, terrible in glorious deeds, doing wonders?' " (Ex. 15:11).

1. What things in these verses show us that God is personal?
2. What do these verses tell us about an infinite God?
3. How can your realizing that God is both personal and infinite help you in your daily life?

Week Two

YOU CAN'T MAKE ME BELIEVE IN A MAKE-BELIEVE GOD

God Speaking

Have you ever tried to talk things over with and get some advice from your dog? That wagging tail could mean "get a different job," "drop algebra," or "break up with Sally." But you know it only means "I like it when you pet me."

Ability to communicate verbally—using a spoken language—is one huge difference between people and animals. Every normal baby in the world can learn to talk. Where did this ability come from? Dogs have not developed it, although there are certainly times they could use it.

It would take a lot of faith to believe that mass, energy, or motion could invent language and enable people to speak it. It seems that only a personal God who wanted to communicate with the people He made, and wanted them to talk with each other, could and would create language.

Without language there is very little communication. If God can't speak to us, we can't really know Him; all of us would have to be agnostics. Those who make fun of the idea of God communicating to people in words forget that it is rather ridiculous to assume that people can do something that their Creator cannot do. But you may be asking, "If God can talk, why doesn't He say something to *me*?" It could be that you are expecting the wrong thing or maybe you are making it impossible for God to speak to you.

Although God has on occasion spoken out loud to people, He usually reveals His will through the *thoughts* He puts into our minds. These are accompanied by a deep inner assurance in our spirits. He also speaks to us through His words in the *Bible*, but even these do not necessarily make sense unless the Holy Spirit explains them to us. For example, the Bible tells you, "Love one another." The Holy Spirit then whispers to your conscience, "That means you'd better love Greg, too."

God can't speak to you if you won't quiet down and listen. Do you ever get away from the TV or turn off the radio in order to find a quiet place to open your Bible and *let* God speak to you? God won't come running after you with a megaphone! You must confess your sin, seek God and sincerely ask Him to tell you what to do. Once you hear His voice, you won't need an intellectual argument to convince you that God can use language. You'll know that it's God speaking.

"The grass withers, the flower fades; but the word of our God will stand for ever" (Isa. 40:8).

"For ever, O Lord, thy word is firmly fixed in the heavens" (Ps. 119:89).

"By faith we understand that the world was created by the word of God" (Heb. 11:3).

"But that same night, the word of the Lord came to Nathan, 'Go and tell my servant David, "Thus saith the Lord . . . " ' " (1 Chron. 17:3, 4).

"It is the Spirit himself bearing witness [showing to be true] with our spirit that we are children of God" (Rom. 8:16).

1. What do these above verses teach us about the words of God?
2. How was the world made?
3. Even though God's Word is so important and so universal, He still speaks to *individuals*. How does God speak to you? What kind of improvements do your "listening habits" need?

The Force Be with You—or Would It Be Better to Have God?

There's an idea found in science fiction such as *Star Wars* which is very interesting—and very dangerous. It's the notion that the whole world is an impersonal unity and that if you can just fit into the "flow" of things and stop working against this force, you will achieve peace and success. If the idea of the world being an impersonal unity is carried to its logical conclusion, it means that God is in everything and everything is God. Instead of having a personal Creator who is above the things He has made, there is a god-force working through all of nature. Instead of the God of the Bible who rules this universe, there is a vague force which makes a tree, a rock, or a cockroach a part of God and a possible object of worship.

The Bible teaches that God is personal and all-powerful. He created everything outside of himself. God is the only One to be worshiped. It is not only silly but sinful to worship a sunset, a majestic mountain, a skunk, a religious leader or yourself. God is not a force to be found in everything, giving you license to worship whatever you please. Just as an artist is separate from the picture he has painted, so God is separate from the people and objects He has made. The artist is above his creation, but his influence and his spirit become part of the picture he has produced, even giving viewers a sense of his presence. In this way the presence of God fills the earth, and the gorgeous sunset and the towering pine tree convey His glory. His attributes are also reflected in the people He has created.

But the painting never equals the painter. Neither does the creation equal its Creator. The most frightening aspect of Pantheism (the belief that God is everything and everything is part of God) is that it teaches that each person is or can become God. Usually terms like "self-realization," enlightenment," "absorption of deity," "illumination," or "union" make this idea sound less ridiculous. Nevertheless, it's the basis of most Eastern religions and of many cults.

Since most people feel weak and insignificant, the idea of being a little god or a part of God is very appealing. It makes the person feel important and powerful. The Bible tells us that we are sinful and that only God can save us. Yet, we are tremendously important, because we are the objects of God's constant love and concern. God offers us the power of the Holy Spirit, not so that we can become God and be worshiped, but so that He can fill us with His presence, and His glory can be reflected through us. We thus fulfill the purpose for which we were created. So you can forget about "the force"—and may *God* be with you.

"They exchanged the truth about God for a lie and worshiped and served the creature [creation] rather than the Creator, who is blessed for ever!" (Rom. 1:25).

" 'Before me no god was formed, nor shall there be any after me. I, I am the Lord, and besides me there is no savior' " (Isa. 43:10, 11).

"It is he who sits about the circle of the earth, and its inhabitants are like grasshoppers; who stretches out the heavens like a curtain, and spreads them like a tent to dwell in; who brings princes to nought, and makes the rulers of the earth as nothing" (Isa. 40:22, 23).

1. According to Romans 1:25, why do people worship nature?
2. What does God say about other "gods"?
3. What's wrong with believing in nature, forces and powers rather than worshiping God?
4. Do you worship a God who is more important than His creation or do you sometimes like to tell God what to do?

Are You Trying to Play God?

Every person wants to understand himself or herself and to answer the question, "Who am I?" That's natural. At first glance it would seem logical that this could be done by looking within yourself. However, the Bible teaches that you best understand yourself by getting to know the God who made you and believing what He has to say about human nature.

Socrates was into a "know thyself" trip. Shakespeare took up the theme with his "to thy own self be true" bit. Some swami has stated, "The inner self of everyone is supreme. It is not sinful."

If you're going to believe that truth is to be found inside *you*, by self-realization, you must believe that you have no sin and that you, not God, are the source of truth. Yet, there are many visible proofs of human sin—the child who suffers because of an alcoholic father, the misfit who is treated cruelly by others, and the people who trample on everyone just to make more money. Unless you believe that the real world is an illusion, you can't possibly consider yourself the ultimate source of truth.

Here's the way Rabi Maharaj, who was a Hindu yogi before he gave his life to Jesus, describes it: "I believed as a Hindu that I was divine . . . that everything was divine. I knew it was impossible for man to become God. So that was my first and major dilemma, not knowing the real God but knowing He was there and not being able to find him in Hinduism. Then . . . as Hindus believed that I was perfect and divine and whereas I tried to believe it with my head, I knew my own imperfections, my own limitations. I did what every good Hindu does to find the truth: I looked into myself. . . . When I looked into myself, I didn't see God. I saw sin."[1]

Believing that the physical world is not real—erasing the difference between reality and fantasy—is the only way that a person can believe that he or she is divine.

The Bible teaches that God is above and apart from the people that He created and that man was made to worship God. You have no right to be in the "God business." You are not divine and you never will be.

Ask the God who made you to run your life and to give you understanding about yourself. It's as sensible as reading the manufacturer's directions instead of asking your alarm clock, "What makes you tick?" You don't have to be another stage failure trying to play God.

"All things were made through him [Jesus, the Word], and without him was not anything made that was made" (John 1:3).

"He [Jesus] knew all men and needed no one to bear witness of man; for he himself knew what was in man" (John 2:25).

1. Why does Jesus know all about you?
2. Why is it wrong to look inside yourself to see who you are and what you were meant to be?
3. Have you ever thanked Jesus for creating you and having a wonderful life planned for you?

The Good Guys and the Bad Guys

Some people don't like the good guys/bad guys approach to religion. They insist that everything in the universe is part of God and that evil doesn't really exist, that evil is only wrong thinking.

The Bible teaches exactly the opposite. In Psalm 50 we read, "The Mighty One, God the Lord, speaks and summons the earth from the rising of the sun to its setting. Out of Zion, the perfection of beauty, God shines forth. . . . He calls to the heavens above and to the earth, that he may judge his people." This teaches that God is perfect, that He is apart from the things He has created, and that He has the right to judge them. The Bible also tells us that there is a devil—and a horde of demons—who are very dangerous. 1 Peter 5:8 warns, "Be sober, be watchful. Your adversary the devil prowls around like a roaring lion, seeking some one to devour. Resist him, firm in your faith."

Yet Christianity is not a belief in dualism with a good god and a bad god. The devil is a fallen angel who was created by God and once was good. In order to do evil, the devil—or any person—must have intelligence and free will (good things created by God). Even though God made all things and rules over them, evil is real and so is the devil.[2] The Bible also teaches that God is much more powerful than the devil so that the person who sticks with God has nothing to fear.

However, if everything is part of God and God is everything in the world, there is no such thing as evil because everything is one and that one is God. This would mean that murdering an innocent baby and giving your hungry friend your last dollar would be equally "God's work." It would mean that you could experiment with

anything you wish because nothing is dangerous. If God is in everything and all is God, there is no danger of being deceived by demons
and evil spirits. The people who trip out on drugs, practice tran-
scendental meditation, and become involved in the occult or in
Eastern religions have to believe that everything is God and that
their visions and voices are not from an evil source.

Christians know better. Christians know that if one lets his
mind go blank or passive, Satan and his demons will be more than
glad to fill it. Therefore a Christian meditates on God's Word and
never allows his mind to remain inactive. He sticks with the Good
Guys—God and His angels—by rejecting evil and actively concen-
trating his mind on God's truth. But, if he blanks out his conscious-
ness, he's giving the bad guys a chance.

"Good and upright is the Lord; therefore he instructs sinners in the way. . . . All the paths of the Lord are steadfast love and faithfulness, for those who keep his covenant and his testimonies" (Ps. 25:8, 10).

"I will meditate on thy precepts, and fix my eyes on thy ways" (Ps. 119:15).

"I revere thy commandments, which I love, and I will meditate on thy statutes" (Ps. 119:48).

"Set your minds on things that are above, not on things on earth. For you have died, and your life is hid with Christ in God" (Col. 3:2, 3).

1. Who is the Source of all good?
2. How do we sinners find God's way?
3. What does God say we should do with our minds?
4. Are you obeying these commands, or does your mind spend much of its free time daydreaming?

Let's Pretend There's a God

Wait a minute! Either there is a God or there isn't. Wouldn't it be better to find out the truth rather than just pretend? Many people, however, are so sure that there are no solid answers that they do live in a pretend world when it comes to religious faith. A famous philosopher by the name of Julian Huxley, for example, suggests that people will function better if they believe in God, even though *he* thinks that no God exists! Another famous guy, a theologian by the name of Kierkegaard, said that one experiences "God" by a "blind leap of faith." In other words, one pretends that God is there. Yet, all of us know that even though pretending can make a person feel better for the moment, it can never solve any real problems.

Jesus, who said, " 'He who sees me sees him who sent me' " (John 12:45) and " 'It is my Father who glorifies me, of whom you say that he is your God' " (John 8:54), claimed to speak the truth about God. He also taught that what Scripture said about God was true. He said, "Scripture cannot be broken" (John 10:35). One can either accept the statements Jesus made or reject them, but in rejecting them one is saying that Jesus lied.

It is interesting to note that the history and makeup of man support Jesus' claim that there is a God who can be known by people.

People from different times and different places have claimed to know God. Anthropologists expect that every group of people has a religion as part of its culture. Not only do we in the twentieth century need to assume that there is a God who makes sense out of life, but throughout history people everywhere have believed in some god and in certain moral obligations. People even go against their own best interests to do the right thing. Firemen routinely risk their lives to save others, and mothers all over the world think of their children before they think of themselves.

Man knows that sin is wrong. People find it easier to commit crimes or other wrong actions at night because they are ashamed to be seen. A teacher can tell who cheated on a test because the usually snotty girl turns into an angel for about a week—to cover the guilt felt from cheating. Obviously, if there was no God, none of this cover-up would be necessary.

It makes sense to conclude that God put the idea of God into man's mind. Termites and elephants aren't concerned with God and morality. Belief in God is one of the most important things that sets man apart from animals. We've discussed the testimony of Jesus and the Bible, the universal awareness of God, and the fact that every person has a conscience. These just might be enough evidence for you to stop pretending and start believing that there is a God.

"He has made everything beautiful in its time; also he has put eternity into man's mind, yet so that he cannot find out what God has done from the beginning to the end" (Eccles. 3:11).

"For the wrath of God is revealed from heaven against all ungodliness and wickedness of men who by their wickedness suppress the truth. For what can be known about God is plain to them, because God has shown it to them" (Rom. 1:18, 19).

1. Where did our questions about God and eternity come from?
2. Can we ever know *everything* about God? Why not?
3. Notice that some basic things about God are very clear to everyone and that we are responsible to live up to what we know. Make a list of the things we know about God and how these should change our lives. (For example: God knows everything, so instead of rationalizing that lie I told my mother, I'd better confess it to her right now.)

Why Isn't God Giving Cash Prizes?

Many people think God should at least give free pizzas, instant answers to algebra problems and cash prizes for good behavior! Others think that since God is love, people should be able to demand from Him whatever they wish. They think God should eliminate hard tests, household chores, arguments and suffering, not to mention war and the rising price of chocolate. However, love is not God's only characteristic, and it is held in balance with His perfect wisdom, knowledge, justice, and holiness, as well as man's free will.

God did not create you to be a programmed robot. You have the ability to talk back to your parents, to put down the kids in your class that nobody likes and to get mad at God. However, God did not create a world without unpleasant consequences for sin. You can't rebel against your parents without becoming a bitter and unhappy person. You can't ignore God's commandments about sex without pain and heartbreak.

But it just isn't fair to blame God for the greed that causes war, the selfishness which prevents the rich from sharing with the poor, and alcoholism which leaves abused children in its wake. It was man's desire always to be right that started the argument.

When the Bible states that God is love, we must remember that its definition of love differs from our sentimental notions. John 14:15 reads, " 'If you love me, you will keep my commandments.' " 1 Corinthians 13:5 says, "Love does not insist on its own way." God showed His love for us by sending Jesus to die for our sins, not by raining Rocky Road ice cream cones from heaven or inventing know-it-all computers so kids wouldn't have to go to school.

God's commandments and His justice are fully consistent with His love; *we* are the ones who have to change our definition of love. When we learn what God's love really is, we'll be glad He doesn't give cash prizes.

"In this is love, not that we loved God but that he loved us and sent his Son to be the expiation for our sins" (1 John 4:10).

" 'Seek the Lord while he may be found, call upon him while he is near; let the wicked forsake his way, and the unrighteous man his thoughts; let him return to the Lord, that he may have mercy on him, and to our God, for he will abundantly pardon' " (Isa. 55:6, 7).

" 'As I live, says the Lord God, I have no pleasure in the death of the wicked, but that the wicked turn from his way and live; turn

back, turn back from your evil ways; for why will you die, O house of Israel?' " (Ezek. 33:11).

1. What plan does God have for us to experience His love and His peace?
2. What is *our* part in this plan?
3. What happens to people who reject God's love shown through His commandments and His sending Jesus?
4. Do you believe God's rules are part of His love for you? Can you thank Him for His commandments?

Indescribable

The feelings following the grand-slam homerun with two out in the last of the eleventh inning, your sister's squeal of delight after Scott's phone call, or the chemistry test that the whole class failed might not be easily described in words. Yet, each of us can relate to all of these experiences. However, describing some of the characteristics or attributes of God is even more difficult, because they are qualities that no human possesses.

God has no physical form but His *actions* show His personality. These actions must be described in words. God is described as having eyes which see good and evil and a mouth which speaks because people understand these terms. Psalm 91 speaks of God as having feathers and wings under which we can take refuge. This does not mean that God is a bird. These words are used only because people can relate to a chick taking refuge under its mother's wings. They can then understand the comfort that God wants to be to us. Similar metaphors describe Jesus as a shepherd, a vine, a roadway, and a loaf of bread.

God has always existed and He is always the same. People just aren't like that. Sometimes the Bible describes things from a human point of view so we can understand better. For example, God sent Jonah to preach to Nineveh so the city would repent. The prophet warned them that their city would be destroyed because of their sin. Although God's unchangeable plan is to reward righteousness and punish wrongdoing, the incident is described in *human* terms: "When God saw what they did, how they turned from their evil way, God *repented* of the evil which he had said he would do to them; and he did not do it" (Jonah 3:10). If you don't keep in mind that the Bible was written in human terminology, this verse may sound as if God, like your father, keeps changing His mind.

It isn't easy to describe God's perfection and the fact that He has always existed and always will. He's *omnipresent*, a big word that means that God is everywhere at the same time. Try to find an example to illustrate that!

Someone has said that the ocean of God's greatness cannot be contained in the bucket of man's mind. However, fill your bucket as full as you can. Study and think about what God is like—and about what He can do for you. God may be indescribable, but He can change your life.

" 'For as the Father has life in himself, so he has granted the Son also to have life in himself' " (John 5:26).

" 'Nor is he [God] served by human hands, as though he needed anything, since he himself gives to all men life and breath and everything' " (Acts 17:25).

"But thou art the same, and thy years have no end" (Ps. 102:27).

" 'For I the Lord do not change' " (Mal. 3:6).

"Before the mountains were brought forth, or ever thou hadst formed the earth and the world, from everlasting to everlasting thou art God" (Ps. 90:2).

" 'Can a man hide himself in secret places so that I cannot see him? says the Lord. Do I not fill heaven and earth? says the Lord' " (Jer. 23:24).

1. List all the characteristics of God you can find in these above verses. Then decide how each should make a difference in your life. (Example: Since God is everywhere, He knows exactly how I act in geometry class, so I'd better shape up.)
2. Have you ever taken five minutes to think of how great God is in comparison with yourself? Why don't you do that right now?

Week Three

IF GOD'S IN HIS HEAVEN, WHAT ON EARTH?

People Are Hard to Figure Out

Do you notice that the football hero who gives such a humble speech at the banquet won't even speak to ordinary mortals in the halls? and that the all-smiles-and-sweetness cheerleader tries to destroy the girl who stole her boyfriend? It seems impossible to truly understand people. You probably don't even understand yourself. You can be so considerate of your girlfriend and so unkind to your mother.

To understand people, we need the knowledge given in the Bible. The Bible teaches that people were created good, but through the sin of Adam and Eve, all people became flawed. "Therefore as sin came into the world through one man and death through sin, and so death spread to all men because all men sinned" (Rom. 5:12). Born without the perfection of Adam and Eve, we're suckers for selfishness—which leads straight to sin.

C. S. Lewis comments, "There are two odd things about the human race. First, that they were haunted by the idea of a sort of behavior they ought to practice, what you might call fair play, or decency or morality, or the Law of Nature. Second, that they did not in fact do so."[1]

A girl may break a promise made to you, but she'll say it's unfair if you break the promise you made to her. People do not equally admire the Nazism of Hitler's Germany and the democracy of the United States. No one thinks that a traitor or a double-crosser is doing the right thing. There is in people's subconscious the idea that God created them to be good. People know there is a right standard of behavior which they are responsible to live up to, but they lack the power to do it.

This is where Jesus Christ comes in. He died and rose again so we could accept Him into our lives to forgive us for the moral laws we've broken *and* to give us power to live up to the standard that God expects of us. People have been ruined by sin, but there is hope for them—in Jesus Christ. People may be hard to figure out, but God wants to take them with all their contradictions and idiosyncracies and remold their lives.

"And God saw everything that he had made, and behold, it was very good" (Gen. 1:31).

"All have sinned and fall short of the glory of God" (Rom. 3:23).

"For as by a man came death, by a man has come also the resurrection of the dead. For as in Adam all die, so also in Christ shall all be made alive" (1 Cor. 15:21-22).

"Therefore, if any one is in Christ, he is a new creation; the old has passed away, behold, the new has come" (2 Cor. 5:17).

1. Why do people sense that they ought to be good, but fail to live up to the highest standard they know?
2. What is the solution to the life of sinfulness that all choose to live?
3. Do you rely on the power of Christ to make you completely new and able to live the way He wants? Or do you still count on your own strength?

Nerds, Wierdos, and Rejects

Many people today consider themselves and others to be zeros. A person is viewed as just a bunch of chemical responses which are predetermined. This means man is a kind of combination robot-zombie. Life, therefore, has no meaning, and people's actions have no significance. If all this is true, good actions and bad actions alike are meaningless; man has no guilt, no responsibility for his actions.

This philosophy might be convenient for those who wish to do wrong, but look at what it does to people and to society. I once toured Colorado State Penitentiary. We listened in on a discussion group for inmates. An intelligent man was serving a life sentence because he had entered a shopping center and shot everybody in sight. He said, "It was just something I had to do." He had no guilt. To him no action had meaning. No country could afford to have many people with his philosophy of life.

If man is a zero, hope, purpose, love, significance, beauty and relationships mean nothing, and man is lost. Yet, we all want these things desperately. Why? Because man has something inside, placed there by the personal God that created him. He is not content being less than a person.

Where do people get the idea that man is a machine or that man is a beast run only by instincts? Of course, if man evolved from slime, energy, apes, or anything else, that is a logical conclusion. And if man is part of some life force—everything is God and God is everything—then man has no personal significance either.

If man was created by a personal God in God's own image, a human being is very valuable. God gave man personality and freedom of choice. Though man is now flawed, his inner sense of hope, love and beauty remind him of what people should be and what they can be in Jesus Christ.

We're not a bunch of nerds, wierdos, and rejects. We're God's special creations. The strawberry malt, horseback riding in the country, the rosy sunset, and the fluffy yellow kitten have meaning as a part of the life God gave you to enjoy.

"So God created man in his own image, in the image of God he created him; male and female he created them" (Gen. 1:27).

"Charge them . . . to set their hopes . . . on God who richly furnishes us with everything to enjoy" (1 Tim. 6:17).

"The earth is the Lord's and the fulness thereof, the world and those who dwell therein" (Ps. 24:1).

"Know that the Lord is God! It is he that made us, and we are his; we are his people, and the sheep of his pasture" (Ps. 100:3).

1. What do these verses tell us about people and the way God cares for them?
2. Do you live as though God created you for *His* special purpose or do you live to please yourself?
3. Do you receive with thankfulness all the things God gives you and do you give Him the credit for all good things?
4. Spend some time thanking God right now.

Illogical Logic

If you've ever memorized some Bible verses, you probably know Proverbs 3:5: "Trust in the Lord with all your heart, and do not rely on your own insight." The Bible is pointing out that all of our education, brilliance and ability to reason are fallible.

We just aren't as smart as we think we are. You've seen the brightest girl use the most illogical statements just to prove her point. You may have realized that during their latest argument, neither of your parents displayed any of the intelligence you know that they both possess.

Man's reason can be corrupted by many things. The salesman who needs money can become blind to all the faults of his product. Many people won't risk embarrassment, loss of prestige, or ridicule, so they lie. Others become so involved in their own ideas that they refuse to listen to anyone else.

Our ability to reason is also warped by things that we have been repeatedly taught. A lot of people believe that man is basically good, just because they've heard it so many times. Yet, an afternoon of baby-sitting with a two-year-old could cure them of this notion.

You're going to have to decide whether you will believe the Bible or trust what your biology text or some famous psychologist says about truth. In making this decision you must realize that all human reasoning can be wrong. Biologists can manipulate experiments to get the results they want, and so can those in other fields of science. The sacred theory of yesterday is thrown out as soon as a new idea comes along.

Remember also that attitudes and opinions of educated and uneducated people alike are affected by many things. Ph.Ds doing research fight with their spouses, carry chips on their shoulders, and hold irrational opinions just like other people do. Educated people also can be prejudiced.

If the greatest scientists can be wrong about their theories of the origin of the universe, perhaps you also can be capable of stretching the truth (Remember the "reason" you gave your mother for needing another pair of Calvin Kleins?).

You may think that your reasoning is fantastic, yet you may be wrong in continuing to date the person your parents have warned you about. God's Word should be the standard which determines the truth of what you study—and don't forget that it is also the yardstick for your own reasoning. All of us are susceptible to illogical logic.

"Then the Lord answered Job out of the whirlwind: 'Where were you when I laid the foundation of the earth? Tell me, if you have understanding. Have you commanded the morning since your days began, and caused the dawn to know its place. . . ? Have the gates of death been revealed to you, or have you seen the gates of deep darkness? Have you entered the storehouses of the snow. . . ? Can you send forth lightnings, that they may go and say to you, "Here we are"? Do you give the horse his might? Do you clothe his neck with strength? Is it at your command that the eagle mounts up and makes his nest on high?' " (Job 38:1, 4, 12, 17, 22, 35; 39:19, 27).

1. How did you do on the above "IQ test" God gave Job?
2. Why is it better to trust God and His Word than the reasoning of humans?
3. Are you being unreasonable and going against God's Word in any area of your life? You'd better pray about it right now.

How Does God Fit into Your Religion?

Why are there so many religions? Religious practices vary from fasting from sunrise to sunset during one month, or dancing all night, to burning oneself alive. But then, shouldn't we expect these if religion is based on man's idea of God? People come from different cultures and different climates; their temperaments are not the same. Therefore, they all see God differently.

It's not surprising that in the overpopulated and undernourished countries of the Orient, the idea of heaven is a nirvana of nothingness. The American Indians conceived the "happy hunting grounds" because in their earthly existence, plenty of game to hunt meant an easy life. Moslems, many of whom come from the hot desert where food spoils quickly, view heaven as a garden where people will eat and drink with good digestion. Founders of some religions had to base their doctrines on very practical considerations. For example, Mohammed included a pilgrimage to Mecca in his religion so the merchants of that city would get back their traditional pilgrimage business—and thus accept the Islamic faith.

Religions can be based on someone's logic, such as that of Confucius, or on people's visions, such as those of Mohammed or Joseph Smith (Mormonism). People tend to fill what Pascal calls the "God-shaped vacuum" by inventing their own gods and their own religious systems. It should be noted here that the devil is very capable of giving people visions and supernatural experiences, but he is not very creative. These religions each have some of the same themes such as good works and rituals. Actions are all-important; sin and the cleansing blood of Christ are not adequately considered. This is not to say that these religions don't have *some* truth in them. Usually there is just enough truth to make people swallow the errors as well.

People can be very sincere—and very wrong. Taking the wrong medicine by mistake won't cure you even if you believe it will. Sincerely believing the gas pedal is the brake pedal won't prevent an accident.

People may be very talented at inventing religions, but they are all like blind people, each describing the small section of the large elephant they feel (one thinks it's like a tree, another thinks it's like a rope).

The only cure for this mess is *revelation*—God breaking into human history and *showing* what the right way is. Jesus Christ did this. By His life, death, and resurrection, He demonstrated that we must "let God be true though every man be false" (Rom. 3:4). Maybe God should have something to do with your religion!

"Now the Spirit expressly says that in later times some will depart from the faith by giving heed to deceitful spirits and doctrines of demons, through the pretensions of liars whose consciences are seared [burned to make dry or hard], who forbid marriage and enjoin abstinence from foods which God created to be received with thanksgiving by those who believe and know the truth. For everything created by God is good, and nothing is to be rejected if it is received with thanksgiving" (Tim. 4:1-4).

1. Where does the Bible say that many religious ideas come from?
2. Why does it seem holy to give up things and be extremely strict?
3. How can you find out what God really wants you to give up and what He wants you to enjoy?
4. Are you willing to trust the Bible rather than the ideas of other people?

Three Billion People Can Be Wrong!

Where do people get this "all religions are good, all lead to God and they're all about the same anyway" idea? It doesn't make sense, because many religions contradict one another. Is it possible to believe that the answer to the test question is A,B,C,D, *and* "None of the above"? Somewhere, we've gotten the idea that it is intolerant and bigoted to say that anyone's religion is wrong or that something in a religion might be false. Yet, 2 + 5 can't equal both 7 and 18. Two contradictory facts cannot both be true.

Every religion except for Christianity says that one merits holiness or peace or paradise by his own good works and ritual keeping. But Christianity says salvation is received as a *free gift* because Jesus died for our sins. After receiving this free gift, people *want* to do works and help others because of what Jesus has done for them. How can the two ideas be true?

Muslims believe that all of one's good deeds will be weighed against the bad ones to determine whether or not a person gets into heaven. This idea is as old as the Egyptian belief in the god Osiris. A modern example of a works religion is Sun Myung Moon's teaching that a convert must bring three spiritual children into the group in order to receive Moon's special blessing for perfection. But the Bible says, "For by grace you have been saved through faith; and this is not your own doing, it is the gift of God—*not because of works*, lest any man should boast" (Eph. 2:8, 9).

In most works religions, it is impossible to have any assurance of salvation—no one can ever be sure he or she has done enough. How different is John's affirmation in the Bible! "I write this to you who believe in the name of the Son of God, that you may *know* that you have eternal life" (1 John 5:13).

The Bible teaches that Jesus is the Son of God who died for our sins and rose from the dead. Islam denies this statement. Both religions cannot be right.

Buddha was an agnostic. He taught that if there was a God, He could not give anyone enlightenment. Every person is on his own. How different from the personal God of the Bible who told Abraham when to move (Gen. 12), who showed Hagar where to find a well (Gen. 21), and delivered Daniel from the lions (Dan. 6).

You can't get by with such sloppy "all religions are the same" thinking and avoid your personal responsibility to search for God. However, if you look *first* for truth in the *Bible*, you'll save a lot of time and trouble. Remember that God is always right and that you—and for that matter, three billion people—can be wrong.

"For all the gods of the peoples are idols; but the Lord made the heavens" (Ps. 96:5).

"As we have said before, so now I say again, If any one is preaching to you a gospel contrary to that which you received, let him be accursed" (Gal. 1:9).

1. What is the biblical position on the argument that "all religions are alike and all are good"?
2. Why should you very carefully test each teaching with the Bible before you accept it?
3. Do you have some religious ideas that don't agree with the Bible? What should you do with those ideas?

That's Life

If you've ever visited your grandfather in the rest home, you may have come home feeling wiped out. How did you react when you heard the eighty-year-old lady calling for her daddy? What did you think when you saw the wrinkled faces and watched your grandfather hobble slowly down the hall with his cane? At first it may have seemed so sad and so cruel. Then you may have had the horrifying thought that sixty years from now you might be like one of these people.

But that's exactly the point. You will not live on this earth forever. God gives you life so that you might accept Christ as your Savior and enjoy His presence now and forever. The sophomore girl who gets leukemia, the baseball pitcher who is crippled by an automobile accident, the homecoming queen who must have her arm amputated, the neighbor man who dies of a heart attack—all remind you that life is finite, that the real purpose of life is to prepare to meet God.

When you see how fragile human life is, you not only realize that you must be ready to die, but that you can't trust in your brilliance and abilities to face life. Putting confidence in your good looks or your physical strength is absurd.

Furthermore, the tragedies of life teach you something about happiness. Joni Eareckson, who lost the use of her arms and legs in a diving accident, shows more zest for life than most people who have no handicaps. She has learned to trust God for her happiness and fulfillment. Since God will always be there and He will never change, she will not be let down.

God shows you every day that man was created to be dependent on God for everything, including fulfillment, peace and contentment, right now as well as for eternity.

The people who meet tragedy with a cynical, "That's life," fail to realize that even with all these none-too-subtle reminders, people aren't really paying attention to God's "That's life, but I'LL give you forever life" advertisements.

"Thus says the Lord: 'Cursed is the man who trusts in man and makes flesh his arm, whose heart turns away from the Lord. He is like a shrub in the desert, and shall not see any good come. He shall dwell in the parched places of the wilderness, in an uninhabited salt land. Blessed is the man who trusts in the Lord, whose trust is the Lord. He is like a tree planted by water, that sends out its roots by the stream, and does not fear when heat comes, for its leaves remain green, and is not anxious in the year of drought, for it does not cease to bear fruit'" (Jer. 17:5-8).

1. Why is it so foolish to trust in your abilities or depend on other people for your security, significance, and happiness?
2. Why is it so easy to depend on yourself and others for these things?
3. Why does trusting God make so much more sense?
4. For what things do you need to start trusting God right now?

Manufacturer's Guarantee

"Man's chief end is to glorify God, and to enjoy Him forever."[2]

But you might interrupt with, "How boring! Isn't the goal of life to have all the fun I can, to fall in love and get married, and to get a good job so I can make lots of money?"

Yet, most people live for these things, and you'll have to admit that they don't seem very content or happy. Besides, doesn't it seem logical to turn to the God who created us to discover the reason for living and the secrets of being truly human, fulfilled, and satisfied?

Because you have sinned your reasoning isn't perfect. The things you think will be so exciting often end up in disaster. The drugs that seem to give so much exhilaration can ruin your life. Even being in love can be pure agony, as you may have already discovered.

But the God who made you knows what will make you happy, even though you don't. Jesus said, " 'For whoever would save his life will lose it; and whoever loses his life for my sake, he will save it' " (Luke 9:24). In other words, the only way to find the complete life God has for you is to give every thought and every action and every possession to Jesus.

The devil has a very successful "big lie campaign" going. The big lie says that if you give your whole life to Jesus, you'll be miserable. Nothing could be farther from the truth. To paraphrase William Law, it's like saying that happiness consists of a mixture of good and bad, of pride and humility, of love for Jesus and selfishness. This is as ridiculous as saying that you'll be happier without a throbbing headache but will enjoy some moderate pain, or that you'll be happier by being partly sick and partly well.[3]

You don't need to sow any wild oats to make your life complete. When Jesus asks you to follow Him completely, He really intends your best happiness. It's just that your logic doesn't understand His ways. You were not made for the constant struggle of defending your own interests and watching out for yourself. You were not created to frantically attempt to work your way to heaven and to prove how good you are. Your Creator intended for you to trust and to obey Him fully and to receive from Him your righteousness. His plan for you is the wonderful relaxation and contentment which comes from handing over the controls of your life to the only One who knows how you can function best.

"What is your life? For you are a mist that appears for a little time and then vanishes" (James 4:14).

"Then Jesus told his disciples, 'If any man would come after me, let him deny himself and take up his cross and follow me. For whoever would save his life will lose it, and whoever loses his life for my sake will find it. For what will it profit a man, if he gains the whole world and forfeits his life? Or what shall a man give in return for his life? For the Son of man is to come with his angels in the glory of his Father, and then he will repay every man for what he has done' " (Matt. 16:24-27).

1. What reasons can you find in the previous verses for giving your life completely to Jesus?
2. Are you willing to give up the logic that says that you should keep certain corners of your life for yourself?
3. Ask God if there is a specific area of your life that He wants you to surrender to Him right now.

Week Four

SCROLLS, SCRIBES, AND CINDERELLA STORIES

Scrolls, Scholars, and a Goat on the Loose

When the "I'm from Missouri" kid says, "Show me the stones that Moses wrote the Ten Commandments on," and, "Show me Isaiah's original scroll, so I can check out his handwriting," what will you say? How do you find out if the Bible we have today is the same as the original books that were written? Here's some help.

Let's imagine a new religion that worships Thomas Jefferson and thinks that the Declaration of Independence is sacred. The followers of this religion spend hours and hours making handwritten copies of the Declaration and even translating it into other languages. Somehow the Jeffersonites lose the original document. How are they going to find out what Thomas Jefferson really said? Obviously, they can compare all the manuscripts. Simple mistakes such as errors in spelling, omissions of words and copying lines twice will easily be spotted; even more complicated mistakes can be cleared up by this method.

This system, which is employed by competent scholars, has been used on the Bible. Until 1947 the oldest Hebrew manuscripts of the Old Testament were only one thousand years old. In 1947 the Dead Sea Scrolls were discovered. Most of these Old Testament manuscripts were written before the time of Christ. Whole books of the Old Testament, such as Isaiah and 1 and 2 Samuel, were found, as well as parts of all the books except Esther. After careful examination, it was found that these manuscripts were essentially the same as the Hebrew manuscripts that were already known. Most of the differences were minor—spelling and punctuation. The fact that the newest versions of the Bible, based on these older manuscripts, have not changed the meaning of anything in the Bible helps prove that we have the same Old Testament that Jesus had. And Jesus taught that the Old Testament was true.

Many scholars were trying to say that the Bible we have today is much different from the one read in ancient times. It was then that God used two little boys, looking for a lost goat, to find a cave hiding clay jars containing the first set of Dead Sea Scrolls. God chose just the right time to show the world that He keeps His Word from being changed.

"He who believes in him will not be put to shame" (1 Pet. 2:6).

"I bow down toward thy holy temple and give thanks to thy name for thy steadfast love and thy faithfulness; for thou hast exalted above everything thy name and thy word" (Ps. 138:2).

1. Do you believe that God, in His timing, will prove that the people who believe the Bible are right?
2. Do you believe that when God asks you to do something hard, He'll take care of the consequences? What is He asking you to do right now?
3. What does God think is the most important thing in the world?
4. What do *you* think is the most important thing in the world? Be honest.

Jesus Put It on the Recommended Reading List

In spite of the fact that many people don't believe the Bible, most have a pretty hard time saying, "I disagree with Jesus," or, "Jesus said that, but He lied." Yet, those who do not accept the truth of the Old Testament must admit one of these two statements, because Jesus believed that the Old Testament was God's Word. In fact, He gave it supreme importance in His life. "The Lord Jesus quoted from at least 24 different Old Testament books," notes Winkie Pratney.[1]

When Jesus was tempted by the devil, He used Bible verses to defeat Satan. One that He quoted was, "Man shall not live by bread alone, but by every word that proceeds from the mouth of God" (Matt. 4:4). He used the Old Testament to confirm His logic, saying, " 'Scripture cannot be broken' " (John 10:35). He assured His listeners, " 'Think not that I have come to abolish the law and the prophets; I have come not to abolish them but to fulfill them. For truly, I say to you, till heaven and earth pass away, not an iota, not a dot, will pass from the law until all is accomplished' " (Matt. 5:17, 18). Jesus agreed with the Pharisees that the Old Testament was the Word of God. The conflict came in matters where they had added their tradition and had given it the same authority as Scripture.

As Jesus walked with two of His disciples on the road to Emmaus, He gave them a Bible study: "And beginning with Moses and all the prophets, he interpreted to them in all the scriptures the things concerning himself" (Luke 24:27). And Jesus had told His Jewish listeners earlier, " 'If you believed Moses, you would believe me, for he wrote of me' " (John 5:46).

Jesus believed biblical events that are now issues of controversy—the stories of Noah and Jonah. He said, " 'For as Jonah was three days and three nights in the belly of the whale, so will the son of man be three days and three nights in the heart of the earth' " (Matt. 12:40), and " 'As it was in the days of Noah, so will it be in the days of the Son of man. They ate, they drank, they married, they were given in marriage, until the day when Noah entered the ark, and the flood came and destroyed them all' " (Luke 17:26, 27).

Maybe the Amalekites, the Amorites, and the Assyrians mix you up a little, and you wonder why the Hebrews were so interested in who a person's great-great-grandfather was, but if you're willing to study and dig a little, you'll find great treasures in the Old Testament. After all, it's the only book Jesus put on His recommended reading list.

" 'Sanctify [make holy] them in the truth; thy word is truth. As thou didst send me into the world, so I have sent them into the world. And for their sake I consecrate myself, that they also may be consecrated in truth' " (John 17:17-19).

"Then he said to them, 'These are my words which I spoke to you, while I was still with you, that everything written about me in the law of Moses and the prophets and the psalms must be fulfilled.' Then he opened their minds to understand the scriptures" (Luke 24:44, 45).

"But he said, 'Blessed rather are those who hear the word of God and keep it!' " (Luke 11:28).

1. What can keep us holy and ready for God's use in a world that tries to pull us away from God?
2. Who opened the minds of the disciples so they *understand* God's Word? Do you ask Jesus to open your mind when you read the Bible?
3. Why is only hearing the Word of God or reading it not enough?

Bratty Brothers and Ancient Manuscripts

If you believe the New Testament, you will have to change your life-style. If the Son of the Maker of the Universe really said, " 'But I say to you that everyone who is angry with his brother shall be liable to judgment' " (Matt. 5:22), then each person has a lot of re-forming to do. There are many reasons for believing that the New Testament is true. Evidence from archeology shows that the New Testament accurately refers to historical events and that it was written when there were still people alive who had known Jesus. William Albright, who was the world's leading biblical archeologist, wrote, "We can already say emphatically that there is no longer any solid basis for dating any book of the New Testament after A.D. 80."[2] F. F. Bruce, a recognized Bible scholar, says, "Archeology has confirmed the New Testament record."[3]

When scholars are checking for copying errors, the more manuscripts that are available to compare and the older they are, the better the chance of finding and correcting any copying errors. Although we don't have the original New Testament manuscripts, we need to realize that the original manuscripts of other historical writings of the time of Christ such as Caesar's *Gallic War* or the *Histories of Tacitus* aren't around either. But there are about *4,000* Greek manuscripts and *8,000* Latin manuscripts (some are not complete) of the New Testament as compared to nine or ten good ones for Caesar's *Gallic War* and two copies of the works of Tacitus. Not only that, but no manuscript of Caesar or Tacitus is earlier than 900 years after these histories were written.

In contrast, there is a scrap from the Gospel of John which is dated A.D. 130. A copy of nearly the whole book of John and three books containing most of the New Testament date less than two hundred years after the death of Christ. A beautiful New Testament manuscript, which is the chief treasure of the Vatican Library, is dated at A.D. 350. No historian ever questions Caesar or Tacitus. Yet, the New Testament is much richer in manuscript evidence than their works are.

When all the New Testament manuscripts are compared, there are very few words that differ. Dr. Palmer of the New York Bible Society asserts that we have reached 98 percent certainty with regards to the New Testament text.[4] F. F. Bruce says, "The variant [different] readings about which any doubt remains . . . affect no material question of historical fact or of Christian faith and practice."[5]

This means that when you read the New Testament, you can be certain that the original did not say, "Everyone who is angry with his brother shall be liable to judgment *unless the kid is a brat*." And it forces you back to square one. Are you willing to let Jesus change your attitude about your little brother or aren't you?

"If any one says, 'I love God,' and hates his brother, he is a liar; for he who does not love his brother whom he has seen, cannot love God whom he has not seen. And this commandment we have from him, that he who loves God should love his brother also" (1 John 4:20-21).

" 'This is my commandment, that you love one another as I have loved you' " (John 15:12).

1. Some people have tried to get out of obeying Jesus by claiming that the New Testament manuscripts are not accurate. What other kinds of rationalizations are there for not obeying verses like those you just read?

2. Have you been trying to get out of loving a particular person?
3. Make a list of the people that you don't love. Ask God's forgiveness and ask Him to give you the love He has for these people.

The Sun Stood Still—Oops!

If the chemistry teacher asks you if you saw the beautiful sunset last night, will you reply, "Don't you even know that the *earth* revolves around the sun? The sun never sets! You're so unscientific that I'll never again believe any formula you teach." All of us know that "sunset" is an expression to describe what *appears* to happen. We even have figures of speech such as "the four corners of the globe," and intelligent people use them! Personification, giving human qualities to something that is not human, is often used in poetry. Even our everyday language is loaded with personifications. We say that a clock has *hands* and that it *runs*. If I want to say "even the sky *cried*" or "the wind *sang* its haunting melody," no one will call me a liar.

Yet, when the Bible uses some of these expressions, people immediately say its unscientific. "A generation goes, and a generation comes, but the earth remains for ever. The sun rises and the sun goes down, and hastens to the place where it rises" (Eccles. 1:4-5) is obviously poetry and not a scientific statement. When Isaiah says, "The mountains and the hills before you shall break forth into singing, and all the trees of the field shall clap their hands" (Isa. 55:12), it doesn't mean that there were mountain choirs and trees with hands in the region where Isaiah lived. Always look for the intention of the author and the context of the statement. Then it is quite easy to identify personification and figures of speech.

On the other hand, it is ridiculous to say such things as, "The Bible says that Jesus walked on the water, but He just knew where the sand bar was"—in one of the world's deepest lakes! It doesn't make sense to say that the account of Adam and Eve is just a nice story to illustrate a truth. Time after time the Bible traces the ancestry of people back to Adam, and the New Testament keeps mentioning him in verses such as, "Yet death reigned from Adam to Moses" (Rom. 5:14).

Avoid interpreting certain verses according to current thinking or selfish desires. The Bible says, "Do not be mismated with unbelievers,"[6] period; not, "Do not be mismated with unbelievers unless you really love each other," or, "Do not be mismated with unbelievers unless the other person promises to go to church with you."

The Bible should be studied with a great deal of prayer, keeping in mind the intention of the writer. If a solar spectacular of the type described in Joshua's day were to be written up today, some author might still write, "The sun stayed in the midst of heaven, and did not hasten to go down for about a whole day" (Josh. 10:13).

"He who dwells in the shelter of the Most High, who abides in the shadow of the Almighty, will say to the Lord, 'My refuge and my fortress; my God, in whom I trust.' For he will deliver you from the snare of the fowler and from the deadly pestilence; he will cover you with his pinions, and under his wings you will find refuge" (Ps. 91:1-4).

"Then the king commanded, and Daniel was brought and cast into the den of lions. The king said to Daniel, 'May your God, whom you serve continually, deliver you!'

"Then, at break of day, the king arose and went in haste to the den of lions. . . . He cried out in a tone of anguish and said to Daniel, 'O Daniel, servant of the living God, has your God, whom you serve continually, been able to deliver you from the lions?' Then Daniel said to the king, . . . 'My God sent his angel and shut the lions' mouths, and they have not hurt me!'" (Dan. 6:16, 19-22).

1. Notice that the Bible can use poetry with figures of speech or use actual history to get the same point across. What is the teaching of the above passages?
2. What snares or lions' dens are you facing now? Ask God to deliver you.

Did God Actually Write the Bible?

God didn't write the Bible down on scrolls and throw them down from heaven. He didn't even dictate it in an audible voice to His mortal secretaries. He used men to write His words, working through their personalities so that each could use his individual style of writing. Because of this, we say the Bible was inspired or "God-breathed." One scholar explains, "By inspiration we mean that holy men of God—under the influence of the Holy Spirit— wrote what God wanted written."[7] And that is quite different from saying that Shakespeare was "inspired" to write great plays or that Mary had a sudden "inspiration."

The view that the whole Bible is the Word of God and that there are no mistakes in it is expressed in the Bible: "All scripture is given by inspiration of God" (2 Tim. 3:16). This was the view of the early Christians and of all churches of all denominations until the eighteenth century. St. Augustine testified, "And when I am confronted in these Books with anything that seems to be at variance with truth, I do not hesitate to put it down whether to the use of an incorrect text, or the failure of the commentator rightly to explain the words, or to my own mistaken understanding of the passage."[8]

Believing that the original scrolls were completely inspired is not begging the question since "only a smattering of textual questions"[9] remain and many of these concern numbers and names, the easiest kinds of copying mistakes to make. Many things that used to be big problems have been solved by knowledge gained from archeology or new scientific discoveries. And we are still learning new things. Like Augustine we should distrust our reason if it doesn't square with the Bible, or wait for new information on the problem.[10]

Obviously, the Bible must quote what people really said and if the person said something that is not true, it must be quoted as such. If a person is quoted as saying something false, or if a figure of speech is used, this is not an error. But a lot of people will tell you that the Bible contains both truth and error. Evidently, each person is to determine for himself what is truth and what is error. Teachers would have a fit if you did that with your textbooks and decided that everything you didn't understand was an error! Doing this with the Bible is preposterous. It makes each person a little god with his or her own system of truth.

You may agree with every word on this page and still try to hedge when the Bible says, "Children, obey your parents,"[11] and, "Do all things without grumbling or questioning."[12] But if all the words in the Bible were put there by God, you'd better obey them.

"Then . . . Johanan the son of Kareah and Azariah the son of Hoshaiah, and all the people . . . came near and said to Jeremiah the prophet, . . . 'Pray to the Lord your God for us . . . that the Lord your God may show us the way we should go. . . . Whether it is good or evil, we will obey the voice of the Lord our God. . . .' When Jeremiah finished speaking to all the people all these words of the Lord their God, with which the Lord their God had sent him to them, Azariah the son of Hoshaiah and Johanan the son of Kareah and all the insolent men said to Jeremiah, 'You are telling a lie. The Lord our God did not send you to say, "Do not go to Egypt to live there" ' " (Jer. 42:1, 2, 3, 6; 43:1, 2).

1. Why didn't Johanan and Azariah want to believe the Word of God?

2. Why are some people so intent on finding errors in the Bible?
3. Is there a verse in the Bible you don't particularly want to obey? Are you trying to say that it's not strictly true?
4. If you've already decided that you are going to move to Egypt, to keep dating Bill or attend the school your parents dislike, why will you find it hard to take God's Word at face value?

Bible Verses and Shopping Trips

Could you imagine living in a world without any Bibles? Although you might at times feel guilty, there would be no final authority telling you not to live with your girlfriend, not to lie to her about the way you feel, or not to eat her for breakfast! Where man came from would be anybody's guess. The purpose of life would be unknown and life after death would be a mystery. Although many live this way because they have not heard about the Bible or they refuse to believe it, the Bible claims to give us the truth on these and many other issues.

The phrase "Thus saith the Lord" can be found in one form or another more than two thousand times in the Old Testament.[13] Examples include: "Then the Lord said to me" (Isa. 8:1), "The Lord spoke to me again" (Isa. 8:5), "Thus says the Lord, the Holy One of Israel" (Isa. 45:11), "And now the Lord says" (Isa. 49:5), and "Then the Lord put forth his hand and touched my mouth; and the Lord said to me, 'Behold, I have put my words in your mouth' " (Jer. 1:9).

The Hebrew people formed the habit of interchanging "God says" and "scripture says." An example can be found in Romans 9:17: "For the scripture says to Pharaoh, 'I have raised you up for the very purpose of showing my power in you, so that my name may be proclaimed to all the earth.' " Paul also shows his belief in the truth of the Old Testament in Romans 15:4: "For whatever was written in former days was written for our instruction, that by steadfastness and by the encouragement of the scriptures we might have hope."

New Testament writers also claimed that God was speaking through their writings. Paul states in 1 Corinthians 14:37, "If any one thinks that he is a prophet, or spiritual, he should acknowledge that what I am writing to you is a command of the Lord."

If Jesus went shopping with you in person, would you pay more attention to what He says than you do to what Bible verses say? Do you take "You shall not covet"[14] seriously, or do you become depressed because you can't buy ten new outfits or get a new Kawasaki? Do you envy your classmate's ski jacket? Do you consider missing church every Sunday to take the job which will enable you to save up for that stereo with the "perfect" sound? Do you take Bible verses like, "There is great gain in godliness with contentment" (1 Tim. 6:6) with you when you're shopping?

"And we also thank God constantly for this, that when you received the word of God which you heard from us, you accepted it not as the word of men but as what it really is, the word of God, which is at work in you believers" (1 Thess. 2:13).

"For the word of God is living and active, sharper than any two-edged sword, piercing to the division of soul and spirit, of joints and marrow, and discerning the thoughts and intentions of the heart" (Heb. 4:12).

1. What do the above verses teach about the power of God's Word?
2. You can prove the Bible's claim to be the Word of God in your own life by believing a verse and obeying it consistently in your life. The change in you is proof of the power of God's Word. Every time you want to complain or feel discontented, try obeying, "There is great gain in godliness with contentment," as the words of God himself. You'll see what I mean.
3. For what situation in your life do you especially need to remember that "there is great gain in godliness with contentment"?

A Real Bible for Real People

How does Esther's risking her life for her people relate to your attitude toward dirty jokes? What does Moses' parting the Red Sea have to do with your geometry test on Tuesday? A lot—if you'll just listen.

The Bible is *relevant*. If God could help David kill Goliath, He can give you the strength to tell your friend about Jesus. If God could give Daniel power to pray in front of His enemies and then deliver him from the lions' den, He surely can help you stand up for what's right when your classmates choose drugs, deceit and defiance. The history in the Bible is a record of God's great actions in the past which show you in the strongest possible way that God can change your life today.

If you were deciding whether or not to take some new cold tablets, which evidence would be most convincing: 1) laboratory experiments that proved the tablets killed germs and viruses; 2) testimony from a person who gained relief from symptoms exactly like yours; or 3) someone's beautiful poem about the merits of the pills? Since rat poison may also kill cold germs and since poetic words don't create reality, you'd be smartest to accept the testimony of the person who really took the pills.

God chose to reveal himself through the experiences of real people, rather than through an erupting volcano which booms, "God is powerful," or through fiction stories with moral value. The Bible shows us how a great big God can relate to people just like us.

God goes to great lengths to show us that His Word is talking about real people who lived in real places and did real things. "The beginning of his kingdom was Babel, Erech, and Accad, all of them in the land of Shinar" (Gen. 10:10) might not seem like the most exciting verse in the Bible, but it clearly shows that God is interested in real places. And one day the archeologists identified the ruins of Erech in the sands of Mesopotamia, further proving that the Bible is accurate in matters of history.

"In the fifteenth year of the reign of Tiberius Caesar, Pontius Pilate being governor of Judea, and Herod being tetrarch of Galilee, and his brother Philip tetrarch of the region of Ituraea and Trachonitis, and Lysanias tetrarch of Abilene" (Luke 3:1) gives the distinct impression that Luke is about to relate something that really happened! And for a long time many people said that Luke made an error because the only Lysanias known in history was the one whom Antony executed to fulfill Cleopatra's wish 36 years before Jesus was born. But a Greek inscription has been found which mentions Lysanias the tetrarch and fits Luke's dating accurately.

The Bible is not a Cinderella story with the moral that good girls get the goodies in the end—if they're pretty. It's a book about a real God for real people.

"Inasmuch as many have undertaken to compile a narrative of the things which have been accomplished among us, just as they were delivered to us by those who from the beginning were eyewitnesses and ministers of the word, it seemed good to me also, having followed all things closely for some time past, to write an orderly account for you, most excellent Theophilus, that you may know the truth concerning the things of which you have been informed" (Luke 1:1-4).

"Now Jesus did many other signs in the presence of the disciples, which are not written in this book; but these are written that

you may believe that Jesus is the Christ, the Son of God, and that believing you may have life in his name" (John 20:30-31).

1. List the reasons Luke and John give for writing their gospels.
2. What statements prove that the information came from people who actually saw the events of the Gospels.
3. In what ways does your believing in Jesus give you life and joy?
4. How can God's acts in history be of help to you today?

Week Five

THE BOOK THAT STARTED THE BESTSELLER LIST

The Age of the Ostrich Is Over

Do you sometimes want to act like an ostrich and hide your head in the sand?

When Ivan the Intellectual puts on his "innocent" sneer and asks, "Do *you* read the Bible and other fairy tales?" does sudden panic grip you? Do you sometimes imagine that a new scientific discovery has just proven the Bible wrong? Or do you have an unshakable faith?

Since the Bible has stood for centuries against constant attempts to discredit it, you have good reason for your faith—even if a current theory or the latest "evidence" seems to disprove the Bible. Anytime the Bible seems to be facing a strong challenge, just wait in faith until all the facts are in. God ably defends himself.

The so-called "truth" in science, psychology and philosophy is always changing. As Paul Little has observed, "Science is a train that is constantly moving."[1] If there is a seeming contradiction between science and the Bible, it's only because all the facts are not yet known. You can wait in faith, for God will show His Word to be true.

It was once stated that the Bible had to be in error because it frequently refers to the Hittites, people who weren't mentioned in any other ancient history. However, in 1906, Hugo Winckler's expedition discovered ruins from the advanced Hittite civilization. This kind of thing has happened many times. "More than 25,000 sites showing some connection with the Old Testament period have been located in Bible Lands."[2] Among these are Ur, the city that Abraham came from; the water tunnel of Hezekiah; and the ashes that Joshua left when he burned Hazor.

"In 1800 the French Institute in Paris issued a list of eighty-two errors in the Bible which they believed would destroy Christianity. Today none of these 'errors' remain."[3] There are difficulties which have not yet been solved, but we need not conclude that there are errors in the Bible.

Nelson Glueck, a Jewish archeologist, said, "No archeological discovery has ever controverted a Biblical reference."[4]

Sir Frederic Kenyon, a former director of the British Museum, writes, "Archaeology has not yet said its last word, but the results already achieved confirm what faith would suggest—that the Bible can do nothing but gain from an increase in knowledge."[5] Would you expect any less from God? Christians don't have to avoid learning for fear that something will contradict the Bible. The Age of the Ostrich is over.

"When I sit in darkness, the Lord will be a light to me" (Mic. 7:8).

" ' "He who believes will not be in haste" ' " (Isa. 28:16).

"Yea, let none that wait for thee be put to shame; let them be ashamed who are wantonly treacherous [purposely evil]" (Ps. 25:3).

"Wait for the Lord; be strong, and let your heart take courage; yea, wait for the Lord!" (Ps. 27:14).

1. If something in the Bible appears contrary to "fact," or if you don't know what to do next, which of the above promises can you claim?
2. Why does demanding an immediate answer or insisting on completely understanding show lack of faith?
3. When you encounter intellectual difficulties in your faith, do you seek the help of others who know more about it than you do? Do you pray in faith expecting an answer? Or do you instantly panic?

4. List the questions you now have. Keep praying that God will show you how to handle these. Also try to find someone, such as your pastor, to help you answer them.

God's Finished Projects

If your world history book says that the Church finally decided which books to include in the New Testament at a council held in Carthage in A.D. 397, don't let the devil throw you a curve. Don't conclude that we probably have the wrong books and that the really good ones have been lost, just because God didn't hand the list down from heaven. Get the whole story.

F. F. Bruce writes, "The historic Christian belief is that the Holy Spirit who controlled the writing of the individual books also controlled their selection and collection, thus continuing to fulfill our Lord's promise that he would guide his disciples into all the truth."[6] Jesus specifically promised that " 'when the Spirit of truth comes, he will guide you into all the truth' " (John 16:13), and that " 'the Counselor, the Holy Spirit, whom the Father will send in my name, he will teach you all things, and bring to your remembrance all that I have said to you' " (John 14:26). That quiet voice of the Holy Spirit continues to speak through the Bible today, converting its readers and giving them the ability to live in a new way.

"For a practical demonstration that the Church made the right choice one need only compare the books of our New Testament with various early documents . . . or even with the writings of the Apostolic Fathers [early church leaders] to realize the superiority of our New Testament books to these others."[7]

Although a few books were questioned for a while, the Church used these criteria to choose their books:

1) *Was it written by an apostle or a close companion of an apostle?* Notice that Peter gives Paul's writings the status of Scripture: "So also our beloved brother Paul wrote to you according to the wisdom given him, speaking of this as he does in all his letters. There are some things in them hard to understand, which the ignorant and unstable twist to their own destruction, as they do the other scriptures" (2 Pet. 3:15, 16).

2) *Was the book used and recognized by most of the churches?*

3) *Did the book teach standard Christian doctrine?*[8]

Although older lists of accepted New Testament books survive, the first Church councils to set up a *"canon"* or official list were held in North Africa, at Hippo Regius in A.D. 393 and at Carthage in

A.D. 397. Bruce reminds us that "the New Testament books did not become authoritative for the Church because they were formally included in a canonical list; on the contrary, the Church included them in her canon because she already regarded them as divinely inspired, recognizing their innate worth, and generally apostolic authority, direct or indirect."[9] The Holy Spirit not only inspired the New Testament authors but guided later Christians to include these books in the Bible.

This is just another history object lesson which shows that God finishes what He starts. When you feel that God could never use you and that you are Exhibit A, "Hopeless, Helpless Christian," remember that God has worked successfully with projects much more complicated than you! His Holy Spirit never fails. Only your resistance to the Spirit can mess things up. If you let the Holy Spirit work in you, some day you'll be one of God's finished projects.

"In him, according to the purpose of him who accomplishes all things according to the counsel of his will" (Eph. 1:11).
"And I am sure that he who began a good work in you will bring it to completion at the day of Jesus Christ" (Phil. 1:6).
"This was according to the eternal purpose which he has realized in Christ Jesus our Lord" (Eph. 3:11).

1. List the things you learn about God's purposes from the above verses.
2. In what ways does it help to know that God will fulfill His purposes even when things look as if they are going the wrong way?
3. Are you willing for God to complete His purpose for you and will you trust Him to do it?

Quoting Hezekiah 6:8 and Other Crazy Things

When Patti Persecutor goes around school telling everybody that the Bible says, "There is no God," just ask for chapter and verse. Then study the Bible for yourself. The words "There is no God" are found in the Bible, but the *whole* verse reads, "The fool says in his heart, 'There is no God' " (Ps. 53:1).

Many argue that the Bible teaches that the world was created in 4004 B.C. Some Bibles do list, in their margins, dates for biblical events. These were figured out by Bishop James Ussher during the seventeenth century. Since we now know that "son" in ancient times was often used to mean descendant and "father" to signify ancestor, we can't necessarily rely on Ussher's dates. Ussher, not God, said that the world was created in 4004 B.C.

Some people are very good at telling others that the Bible says things it does not say or at quoting statements out of context. Many verses in the book of Ecclesiastes are often taken out of context. The writer of this book tells of the intellectual struggles of his life. At one point in his life he believed that death was nothingness and that the most important thing in life was enjoyment. At the end of his life he sees the importance of God and therefore changes his viewpoint. He says, "Because man goes to his eternal home . . . and the dust returns to the earth as it was, and the spirit returns to God who gave it. . . . The end of the matter; all has been heard. Fear God, and keep his commandments; for this is the whole duty of man. For God will bring every deed into judgment, with every secret thing, whether good or evil" (Eccles. 12:5, 7, 13, 14). The entire book must be studied to understand any one of its verses.

When Irwin the Irresponsible says, "*I* heard, that *he* said, when *he* quoted the world's greatest authority, that the *Bible* says. . . ," ask him to show you *where* the Bible says it. Remember also that there are altered versions of the Bible around. Since the major versions have all been translated by competent scholars from ancient manuscripts in the original languages, there is no place for a Bible which contradicts all other versions.

By the way, laziness is a sin and we are commanded to *study* God's Word. Many young people have landed in strange cults because they were too lazy to investigate what the Bible really says and seriously study it. You should know that Hezekiah is not a book of the Bible and that "Do your own thing" is not a Bible verse.

"Now these Jews were more noble than those in Thessalonica, for they received the word with all eagerness, examining the scriptures daily to see if these things were so" (Acts 17:11).

"For Ezra had set his heart to study the law of the Lord, and to do it, and to teach his statutes and ordinances in Israel" (Ezra 7:10).

" 'And these words which I command you this day shall be upon your heart; and you shall teach them diligently to your children, and shall talk of them when you sit in your house, and when you walk by the way, and when you lie down, and when you rise' " (Deut. 6:6-7).

1. List all the requirements for knowing and understanding God's Word.

2. Are you willing to exert as much energy in studying God's Word as you do in fixing up your car or putting on your makeup?

3. Are you determined to study God's Word as Ezra did?

Do You Need a Degree from Whale Seminary?

"So a fish swallows Jonah, Jesus walks on the water, and the Red Sea opens just in time, making a spectacular splash for the Miracles on Water Show. Does God do as well on land?" Faithless Freddy may even have more to say, but at least he has one issue straight—one's concept of God determines his attitude toward miracles. If one really believes in an all-powerful Creator God, he believes that God could "minnowize" that big fish so Jonah could swallow the whale!

Someone has described miracles as "unusual events caused by God."[10] Actually, everyday occurrences also caused by God and our so-called laws of nature are only descriptions of what normally happens. The law of physics and chemistry, for example, give no cause behind the things we can observe.

There are some good historical reasons for believing the miracles of the Bible. It is interesting that non-biblical sources mention the miracles of Jesus, and His enemies do not deny them. Josephus, a Jewish historian of the first century, calls him a wonderworker. Later Jewish religious writings say He did His miracles by black magic. This is also the explanation given by Celsus, a philosopher who criticized Christianity in the second century.[11]

All of our historical sources agree that Jesus did miracles. Paul Little notes that although people who see something happen may give conflicting reports, we still use the testimony of eyewitnesses in court—even to convict people of murder—and the system works. The circumstances surrounding the miracles of Jesus give stronger evidence for believing them:

1) They were done in public.

2) Some were performed in the presence of nonbelievers.

3) Jesus' miracles were done over a period of time and involved a variety of powers: healing the blind, calming the storm, and raising the dead. He didn't rely on one Houdini trick.

4) There were testimonies from cured people.

5) Biblical miracles have an order, purpose and dignity which are lacking in the miracles claimed by pagan religions. "We have discussed the historical reliability of Bible records. Similar investi-

gations into pagan records of miracles would soon show there is no basis for comparison."[12]

Bible miracles have a purpose. God gets concerned if His people disobey Him. Take Jonah, for instance. His degree from Whale Seminary made him obedient and showed the world forever that it's a big deal when a person boards a ship for Tarshish if God has told him to go to Nineveh.

"Then Jonah prayed to the Lord his God from the belly of the fish, saying, 'I called to the Lord, out of my distress, and he answered me; out of the belly of Sheol I cried, and thou didst hear my voice. The waters closed in over me, the deep was around about me; weeds were wrapped about my head at the roots of the mountains. Those who pay regard to vain idols forsake their true loyalty. But I with the voice of thanksgiving will sacrifice to thee; what I have vowed I will pay. Deliverance belongs to the Lord.' And the Lord spoke to the fish, and it vomited out Jonah upon the dry land" (Jonah 2:1, 2, 5, 8, 9, 10).

1. Rewrite Jonah's prayer in your own words.
2. Have you ever had a Jonah-and-the-whale experience in which God showed you that disobeying Him was not worth the trouble?
3. Notice that Jonah determines to keep his promises to God *with thanksgiving*. If God is asking you to do something hard, determine to obey with thanksgiving.

No Uncertain Future

When your grandmother smiles and tells you, "You're young and you have your whole life before you," do you remember overhearing her say, "I'm glad I didn't have to grow up in times like these"?

Do you mumble to yourself, "Thanks a lot for what you've left the younger generation. I'll probably fight in World War III"?

If you have doubts about the future, you might be interested in the Bible's track record in predicting it.

One of the most interesting and exciting proofs that the Bible is the Word of God is that of fulfilled prophecy. Biblical predictions have been fulfilled in amazing ways. We'll consider some of God's promises concerning the land of Israel.

God said to Abraham in Genesis 17:8, " 'And I will give to you, and to your descendants after you, the land of your sojournings [wanderings], all the land of Canaan, for an everlasting possession;

and I will be their God.' "

Ezekiel, who prophesied over five hundred years before the birth of Christ, said, " 'For thus says the Lord God: Behold, I, I myself will search for my sheep, and will seek them out. As a shepherd seeks out his flock when some of his sheep have been scattered abroad, so will I seek out my sheep; and I will rescue them from all places where they have been scattered on a day of clouds and thick darkness. And I will bring them out from the peoples, and gather them from the countries, and will bring them into their own land; and I will feed them on the mountains of Israel, by the fountains, and in all the inhabited places of the country" (Ezek. 34:11-13).

For a long time these prophecies seemed impossible. The land of Palestine was part of the Turkish Empire. Jews were not welcome. The idea of a Jewish state seemed ridiculous. But after Hitler slaughtered six million Jews, the members of the United Nations voted to allow a Jewish state. Many of the prophecies about the Jews and Israel have not yet been fulfilled. But the incredible story of the 1948 war in which Israel defeated the united Arab nations, in order to keep her land, should be enough to prove to anybody that God's Word will stand true no matter what the odds are.

Careful study of the Bible will convince you of God's great plan as it has been fulfilled in history and as it relates to the future in prophecy that is yet to be fulfilled. Neither the number of missiles possessed by the Soviet Union nor the newest world crisis need alarm you. God is in control of each nation and of all future events. For those who've given their lives to Jesus and who study their Bibles, there is no uncertain future.

"Let the heavens be glad, and let the earth rejoice, and let them say among the nations, 'The Lord reigns!' " (1 Chron. 16:31).

"For dominion belongs to the Lord, and he rules over the nations" (Ps. 22:28).

"For God is the king of all the earth; sing praises with a psalm! God reigns over the nations; God sits on his holy throne" (Isa. 47:7-8).

1. What promises in the above verses can help you when it looks as if World War III is about to break out?
2. What things about the future scare you most? Talk these things over with God and find Bible promises to claim so you can deal with your fears.
3. Why can you praise God when you think of the future? Do you ever thank God for the future He's planned for you?

I Did My Book Report, but . . .

Have you ever sneaked into the football game by saying that your buddy inside has your money and you'll be right out to pay? Or told your father he's too old-fashioned to understand anything? Or given a false excuse for not handing in your book report on time? If you have, you have collided directly with commandments of the Bible, such as "Owe no one anything, except to love one another" (Rom. 13:8), "Honor your father and your mother" (Ex. 20:12), and "Do not lie to one another, seeing that you have put off the old nature with its practices" (Col. 3:9).

The Bible's claim to absolute truth for all people, everywhere, for all time, is not very popular in our do-your-own-thing-if-it-feels-good-do-it society. But then neither is anything or anyone who keeps people from doing exactly what they wish to do at any particular moment. *Popularity, however, does not determine truth.*

Even common sense tells you that people can't be happy if they are continually trying to steal from each other and lie to each other. Leaving the decision to each individual to "do the best thing in the given situation" is a frightening prospect. Consider how easy it is to rationalize selfishness in order to save face. It should come as no surprise that the God who made us knows the rules by which we best operate and by which people best relate to each other.

The Bible not only tells us the rules by which to live; it explains how we each can be transformed by the power of the Holy Spirit so that God can fulfill these laws in us.

The book, *Valley of the Kwai*, by Ernest Gorden beautifully shows how this worked in a tough situation. Gorden had been imprisoned by the Japanese on the Malay Pennisula during World War II. The starving prisoners, who were stealing from each other and living almost like animals, decided to read the New Testament together. These skeptics came to trust in Christ, who gave them power to obey the commandments of the New Testament and to have genuine love for each other.

Can you honestly thank God for all His rules, even the ones that are hard to obey? When you're tempted to say, "I did my book report, but my little sister used it for her finger painting," thank God for His commandment and say, "I didn't finish my book report because I put it off until the last minute. It's my fault." That kind of obedience will bring you freedom and joy which will convince you of the wisdom of God's commandments.

"I will delight in thy statutes; I will not forget thy word" (Ps. 119:16).

"Thy testimonies are my delight, they are my counselors"
(Ps. 119:24).

"I will keep thy law continually, for ever and ever; and I shall walk at liberty, for I have sought thy precepts. . . . I find my delight in thy commandments, which I love. I revere thy commandments, which I love, and I will meditate on thy statutes" (Ps. 119:44, 45, 47, 49).

1. What attitudes does the Psalmist have toward God's commandments?
2. What must a person believe about God in order to really love every commandment He gives?
3. What attitude do you have toward God's commandments? Maybe you'd better pray about the commandments you don't appreciate.

Do You Have the Whole Picture?

Some people criticize the Bible because they don't like its moral absolutes. The unpopularity of the Ten Commandments stems, not from the idea that obeying them would produce a bad society (it's easy enough to see that they are wonderful laws for any group of people), but from the fact that people know they can't live up to them. It's easier to criticize than to admit weakness. It sounds good to say that there are situations in which it would be better not to tell the truth. Yet, if I think it's my right to decide when I will tell the truth and when I will lie, I am no longer trustworthy.

The beauty of the life God wants to give us—the life described in the Bible—is that God offers us power from outside of ourselves to obey His commandments. When we repent of our sins and completely turn our lives over to God, the Spirit of Jesus comes to live in us and give us power. The Apostle Paul describes it this way: "I have been crucified with Christ; it is no longer I who live, but Christ who lives in me; and the life I now live in the flesh I live by faith in the Son of God, who loved me and gave himself for me" (Gal. 2:20). When Christians fail, it's because they turned off the power switch, not because God's laws are too strict.

Many find another problem. They assume that those who try to live by all the commandments of the Bible have no love for those who don't. They assume that only those who disregard the commandments can have sympathy for other people. But if you study the Bible carefully, you'll realize that the Holy Spirit not only wants to give us *power* to obey God's laws, but He also wants to supply us with *love* and compassion for people who are doing wrong things. Jesus was harder on the hypocrisy of the Pharisees than on the immorality of the woman at the well. Yet, He made it clear that both needed to change.

The people whose motto is, "The sins I don't commit are the worst," don't take seriously what the Bible has to say about pride and self-righteousness. With the power of the Holy Spirit it is possible to hate sin and love the sinner (but that doesn't mean condoning his sin). The robber may tell you that you can't really love him unless you accept his thievery, and the four-year-old may say, "You don't love me," when you take away the knife he wants to play with, but that doesn't change the truth. Real love is based on moral absolutes, not on encouraging people to do wrong.

People who only know the "Thou shalt nots" of the Bible, whether they disobey them or try to ram them down the throats of everyone else, have only half the picture. The whole picture includes the power of the Holy Spirit to obey God and to love those who don't, because God loves them.

"Therefore, my beloved, as you have always obeyed, so now, not only as in my presence but much more in my absence, work out your own salvation with fear and trembling; for God is at work in you, both to will and to work for his good pleasure" (Phil. 2:12-13).

" 'But I say to you, Love your enemies and pray for those who persecute you, so that you may be sons of your Father who is in heaven; for he makes his sun rise on the evil and on the good, and sends rain on the just and on the unjust' " (Matt. 5:44-45).

" 'God chose to make known how great . . . are the riches of the glory of this mystery, which is Christ in you, the hope of glory' " (Col. 1:27).

1. Where does the power to obey God come from?
2. What is the Source of the power to love everyone?
3. Are you depending on the Holy Spirit or trying to obey God's rules in your own strength?
4. How can you "hate sin and love the sinner"?

Week Six

THE FACTS ABOUT CHRISTMAS

Worth Celebrating

Suppose someone asks you, "Why do you celebrate the pagan festival of Christmas? Don't you know that December 25 was once a Roman holiday?" How will you answer?

No one knows the date of Christ's birth. And it is true that several pagan festivals took place on December 25, which by the old calendar was winter solstice, the shortest day of the year. Nevertheless, there are some good reasons for having a special occasion to remember the birth of Jesus.

First, the Old Testament pattern was to celebrate God's great acts in history. The Sabbath reminds us of God's resting after the six days of creation. Passover commemorates the deliverance of the Israelites. Purim remembers Queen Esther's heroic saving of the Jews in the Medeo-Persian Empire. Jesus apparently took part in all the Jewish feasts which celebrated the work of God in history.

Second, an important biblical principle states, "Do not be overcome by evil, but overcome evil with good" (Rom. 12:21). An evil festival can be changed into a good one. During December, the Romans celebrated Saturnalia, a feast in honor of Saturn, the god of agriculture. People of Europe set bonfires on December 25 to remind the sun to return; by the fourth century, followers of Mithraism were celebrating December 25 as the birthday of the Unconquered Sun; Northern Europeans kept this time as sacred to Wodin (Odin). With all the world celebrating, Christians felt that this would be a good time to remember the birth of Christ who came to save us from sin and give us eternal life. They apparently adapted some of the existing customs by giving them Christian meaning. The evergreen tree, for example, was often used in the pagan festivals. However, it seemed a natural symbol of the eternal life, so it eventually became part of the Christmas celebration.

It is plain to see that some of the ways in which people today celebrate Christmas are not right. However, it is better to discard the evil and keep the good rather than to throw out the baby with the bath water. One of the tactics of the devil is to convince people that anything fun is wrong and that we can make ourselves righteous by giving up all kinds of things. But God, who programmed birds to give concerts and monkeys to put on free comedy shows, certainly wants us to enjoy many things. He doesn't want our lives loaded down with strict rules and prohibitions. He wants us to enjoy living under His guidance, having all our activities purified by our obedience to Him. As you read the Old Testament, you'll see that the feasts were times of fun and celebration. Shouldn't the birth of Jesus be the most enjoyable celebration of all?

"And Nehemiah, who was the governor, and Ezra the priest and scribe, and the Levites who taught the people said to all the people, 'This day is holy to the Lord your God; do not mourn or weep.' For all the people wept when they heard the words of the law. Then he said to them, 'Go your way, eat the fat and drink sweet wine and send portions to him for whom nothing is prepared; for this day is holy to our Lord; and do not be grieved, for the joy of the Lord is your strength.' So the Levites stilled all the people, saying, 'Be quiet, for this day is holy; do not be grieved.' And all the people went their way to eat and drink and to send portions and to make great rejoicing, because they had understood the words that were declared to them" (Neh. 8:9-12).

1. Why were the Israelites told to celebrate and enjoy the day?
2. Do you thank God for good times, share your fun with Him and use your joy as a means of worshiping God?
3. What are straight-laced, sober and sad Christians missing?

The Greatest Christmas Gift

The celebration of Christmas focuses on the biblical truth that Jesus was both human and divine. The account of the birth of Jesus shows clearly the two natures of Christ. It contradicts heresies (false beliefs) that are still around today in many forms. One such heresy is called Gnosticism. The Gnostics said that Jesus was never truly human and that He did not have a real body. Another heresy called Arianism taught that Jesus was neither God nor man but a specially created being with more power than man and less power than God. Other heresies claimed that Jesus was only a good person.

The Bible vividly shows the humanity of Jesus—a little helpless baby, born of a human mother, bundled up in a musty feed trough. The animals in His nursery were not on the wallpaper! It was all very real and *very* human. John summed it up by writing, "And the Word became *flesh* and dwelt among us" (John 1:14).

Yet, in no way was Jesus less than God. Mary was promised, " 'He will be great, and will be called the Son of the Most High; and the Lord God will give to him the throne of his father David, and he will reign over the house of Jacob for ever; and of his kingdom there will be no end' " (Luke 1:32-33). This prediction could not be describing a mere human being.

Isaiah's prophecy was fulfilled: "For to us a child is born, to us a son is given; and the government will be upon his shoulder, and his name will be called 'Wonderful Counselor, *Mighty God, Everlasting Father*, Prince of Peace' " (Isa. 9:6). The wise men *worshiped* Jesus rather than Mary or Joseph.

Most people who despise Christmas refuse to believe that Jesus was fully human and fully divine. They are uncomfortable with the baby in the manger who was worshiped by the wise men. Understandably, the fact that Jesus was "born in the likeness of men" (Phil. 2:7) *is* incredible. Why would God, who created all things, place himself in the position of being fed and cared for by a human mother? Jesus showed us, by becoming human and dying for us that His love has no equal, even in the imagination of man. Jesus was born in Bethlehem so that He can be born in the heart of every person who accepts the first and greatest Christmas gift.

"Have this mind among yourselves, which you have seen in Christ Jesus, who, though he was in the form of God, did not count equality with God a thing to be grasped, but emptied himself, taking the form of a servant, being born in the likeness of men. And being found in human form he humbled himself and became obedient unto death, even death on a cross. Therefore God has highly exalted him and bestowed on him the name which is above every name, that at the name of Jesus every knee should bow, in heaven and on earth and under the earth, and every tongue should confess that Jesus Christ is Lord, to the glory of God the Father" (Phil. 2:5-11).

1. List the things in these verses which clearly teach that Jesus is God.
2. Explain in your own words the cost involved in giving the "first" Christmas gift.
3. Have you accepted that gift?
4. Ask God to show you the ways in which you don't have the attitude and mind of Jesus.

If Christ Had Not Come

When you read in your history book that Christ was born in 4 B.C. (some books say 5 B.C.), you might be interested in learning some facts about chronology. People often date things relative to major events—a big flood, the beginning of a king's reign, or in the case of the Jewish calendar, the exodus of the Hebrews from Egypt. Actually, a Scythian monk named Dionysius Exiguus, who lived from A.D. 496 until 540, began the practice of numbering our years according to the birth of Christ. It all began while he was preparing a chart to show the correct method of calculating the date of Easter. Because he didn't want to reckon time according to the reign of a pagan ruler, he numbered years according to the birth of Christ. This method was gradually adopted in different countries and was in general use in Europe by the eleventh century. The rest of the world eventually accepted it as well.

Actually, Dionysius made a mistake in his calculations. His dating system was questioned as early as the eighth century by an Englishman named Bede. "Nevertheless it has continued in use to the present day, and as a result the nativity is reckoned to have taken place in or shortly before the year 4 B.C. when Herod died."[1] Every copy of the modern calendar points to the birth of Christ as the great turning point of history.

After Christ came, nothing could ever be the same again. There was the standard of His perfect life—the Life by which every life must now be measured. There was the fact of His victory over death. The resurrection meant that people could face death with confidence and serenity.

Christ's coming also means that each person has to accept Christ or reject Him, to be for Him or against Him. You can't mention the name of Jesus Christ and get a neutral response. More than the manger scene on your piano would be missing if Christ had not come. Imagine a world without churches, New Testaments and Christian music. Hope would be gone.

But Jesus did come and He came for you. He offers you hope—hope of a forever in heaven where "death shall be no more, neither shall there be mourning nor crying nor pain"[2] for those who give their lives to Jesus completely. But there's also hope for *today*. Jesus came to give you love that no one else has for you. He came so you'd have someone to guide you through all the confusion. He has hope for you, even if your parents are getting a divorce, even if you feel like the most unpopular kid at school, and even if you're tempted to go back to drugs. Don't live as if Christ had not come. He came—to stay with you forever.

" 'Lo, I [Jesus] am with you always, to the close of the age' " (Matt. 28:20).
" 'For where two or three are gathered in my name, there am I in the midst of them' " (Matt. 18:20).
"Grace to you and peace from God our Father and the Lord Jesus Christ" (2 Cor. 1:2).

1. When do you find it easy to forget that Jesus is with you?
2. Do you ask Jesus for His love, His grace and His peace, or do you slug it out on your own?
3. Thank Jesus right now that He has love, grace, peace and hope for you.

The Outstanding Teenager Award

In my opinion a young girl who grew up in Nazareth was the most outstanding teenager that ever lived. Bible scholars who have studied ancient Jewish customs all seem to agree that Mary gave birth to Jesus when she was still in her teens. But Mary was no haloed angelic being. She was made out of the same stuff as any other teenaged girl. The difference was that her commitment to God had no reservations. She is the finest example of a godly young person. But think a moment of the cost of her commitment.

How many engaged girls would welcome the angel's message: "Behold, you will conceive in your womb and bear a son"? Mary knew full well that this might mean giving up Joseph, though she must have loved him very much. How would Joseph react to her being pregnant? After all, she could hardly expect him to believe the story about the angel. Then what would her parents and the people of the village think? The town gossips would certainly give the story headline coverage! Mary would have to give up her reputation as the nicest girl in Nazareth. Even if Joseph would believe her, people would think that she and Joseph had to get married. She even gave up her right to her own body. She didn't ask for two more years to enjoy her freedom before settling down to the responsibilities of parenthood.

But that was not all. The law of Moses stipulated that a bride who was not a virgin should be stoned by the men of the village. Mary was risking her life.

Mary had complete trust in God. Her only question, " 'How can this be, since I have no husband?' " revealed, not only her sanity, but also her willingness to let God have His way. She would not try to arrange a quick marriage to Joseph so that she could bear a son. Mary had perfect faith in God—faith that God would take care of all the consequences if she obeyed, and He did. If God is asking you to surrender something in your life, let the example of Mary give you the courage to obey God fully and trust Him with the outcome.

"And the angel said to her, 'Do not be afraid, Mary, for you have found favor with God. And behold, you will conceive in your womb and bear a son, and you shall call his name Jesus.' And Mary said to the angel, 'How can this be, since I have no husband?' And the angel said to her, 'The Holy Spirit will come upon you, and the power of the Most High will overshadow you; therefore the child to be born will be called holy, the Son of God. For with God nothing will be im-

possible.' And Mary said, 'Behold, I am the handmaid of the Lord; let it be to me according to your word' " (Luke 1:30, 31, 34, 35, 37, 38).

1. What is the difference between *asking questions* about God's will and *questioning* God's will?
2. Someone has said, "Every 'how' question in the spiritual life has the same answer—'The Holy Spirit.' " Why is this true?
3. Are you willing to say "yes" to God on some issue now and to trust the Holy Spirit to accomplish it through you?

A Love Story

Many people recite the biblical teaching as stated in the Apostles' Creed, "Conceived by the Holy Spirit, *born of the virgin Mary.*" But is a virgin birth logical? There were, after all, plenty of Roman soldiers around; or maybe Joseph and Mary covered up their sin of premarital sex by inventing a story. Some contend that people who wanted a divine Jesus came up with a good nativity scene in order to sell their book. After all, the Greek gods were always having human children; some sources say that even Alexander the Great (who lived nearly three hundred years *before* Jesus) was taught by his mother that he was the son of a god. But then, does it actually matter whether or not Jesus was born of a virgin? Isn't it just His good life that counts anyway?

Yes, it does matter. It is crucial. If God the Holy Spirit is not the Father of Jesus, then Mary was a very sinful woman, for not only did she commit fornication, but she continually lied to cover it up. If Jesus was not born of a virgin, His teaching is false and statements such as " 'You are from below, I am from above; you are of this world, I am not of this world' " (John 8:23), and " 'If God were your Father, you would love me, for I proceeded and came forth from God' " (John 8:42) would be lies. If Jesus were a liar, He could not die for our sins, because He would have to die for His own.

People in Jesus' time were not so primitive and gullible that they'd believe anything. They knew very well how babies are made. They certainly didn't expect an event like this. The God of the Hebrews was the "high and lofty One who inhabits eternity" (Isa. 57:15) and not some Apollo or Zeus who kept dropping in to visit beautiful women. The people of Nazareth knew Mary and Joseph personally and they watched Jesus grow up. They knew He was human. Yet, the whole life of Jesus, as well as His miracles and His resurrection, confirmed that He was no ordinary mortal.

Some who doubt the biblical account of the birth of Jesus won't accept the possibility that Mary and Joseph could exercise so much purity, self-control and sacrificial love. Joseph never considered side-stepping God's law to marry the girl he loved. He was planning to break up with her quietly in order to cause a minimum of pain. But God wanted him to take Mary as his bride and He sent an angel to tell Joseph. So Joseph "did as the angel of the Lord commanded him. He took his wife, but knew her not [had no sexual intercourse] until she had borne a son" (Matt. 1:24, 25).

The devil tells you, "If you really love somebody, you just can't help but have sex with that person." But God promises the unlimited power of the Holy Spirit to all His *obedient* children in order to live pure lives, just as Mary and Joseph did. Their love story, full of faith and sacrifice, made possible the Greatest Love Story of all: "For God so loved the world that he gave his only Son."[3]

"Now the birth of Jesus Christ took place in this way. When his mother Mary had been betrothed to Joseph, before they came together she was found to be with child of the Holy Spirit; and her husband Joseph, being a just man and unwilling to put her to shame, resolved to divorce her quietly. But as he considered this, behold, an angel of the Lord appeared to him in a dream, saying, 'Joseph, son of David, do not fear to take Mary your wife, for that which is conceived in her is of the Holy Spirit; she will bear a son, and you shall call his name Jesus, for he will save his people from their sins.' When Joseph woke from sleep, he did as the angel of the Lord commanded him; he took his wife, but knew her not until she had borne a son; and he called his name Jesus" (Matt. 1:18-21, 24-25).

1. Are you, like Joseph, willing to obey God in everything He commands?
2. Are you receiving the power of the Holy Spirit which enables you to obey God?

Wise Men's Gifts—from a Department Store!

After four hours of frantic Christmas shopping, you discover that not one store in the city has the long-sleeved pink blouse which your sister wants. You're ready to believe anything—even the spiel which says giving gifts at Christmas comes from the pagan feast of Saturnalia and is therefore most sinful. It is true that during the Roman celebration of Saturnalia, the rich gave gifts to the poor. It is also true that the Church at first feared that giving gifts at Christmas would make it too much like the pagan holiday. Christmas gift-giving did not become popular until the twelfth century.

The giving of Christmas gifts *can* be wrong. It is not right for you to purchase presents in a frantic tizzy, in mortal fear that your family and friends won't like what you purchased. Spending extravagantly, just to be well thought of, reflects impure motives.

Receiving gifts can be just as wrong. If you're more concerned about the gifts you get than the love behind them, something isn't right. The handkerchief from Aunt Tillie and the old-fashioned mittens from Grandpa shouldn't fill you with disappointment.

Whether Christmas gift-giving is pagan or truly Christian depends on *heart attitudes*, not on the custom itself. Do you take God with you when you shop and do you pray about the presents you buy? Ask Jesus how much money to spend and how to organize your time. Pray for each person on your shopping list and ask God to help you love that person, as well as to help you choose the appropriate gift for him or her. After you've done all these things, leave the reaction of the people in God's hands. If your dad doesn't even say thank-you for the slippers, you can trust Jesus and not feel hurt.

Learn also to be thankful for each thing you receive. A spirit of thankfulness is not only an asset to your personality, but a command of God. And remember, it was Jesus himself who said, " ' "It is more blessed to *give* than to receive" ' " (Acts 20:35). The wise men gave Jesus gold, frankincense and myrrh.

Maybe you'd like to give Jesus a birthday present too. You may have heard the well-known story about the old man who invited everybody to his birthday party only to be completely ignored while the guests exchanged gifts among themselves. That might sound like Christmas at your house, but you may not know what to do about it. Well, Jesus said, "As you did it to one of the least of these my brethren, you did it to me" (Matt. 25:40). Christmas is a wonderful time to show love to the lonely neighbor lady, the man in the rest home, or the kid at school who has no friends. Wise men's gifts have no selfish motives.

"He who is kind to the poor lends to the Lord, and he will repay him for his deeds" (Prov. 19:17).

"You will be enriched in every way for great generosity, which through us will produce thanksgiving to God" (2 Cor. 9:11).

"Each one must do as he has made up his mind, not reluctantly or under compulsion, for God loves a cheerful giver" (2 Cor. 9:7).

1. What is our way of giving to Jesus?
2. What does the Bible have to say about generosity?
3. Ask God how your Christmas giving, and your use of money in general, could give more glory to Him.

Did You Miss Christmas?

The twenty-fifth of December is on the calendar every year. But tree-decorating, eating turkey dinner, carolling, attending church, or even giving to the Salvation Army won't guarantee that anything at all will happen inside you.

The first Christmas happened only to those whose hearts were ready to receive the Christ that God had sent—a humble and God-fearing couple, simple shepherds, an old man named Simeon, a praying woman called Anna, and wise men who thought that eternity was more important than time. Being ready wasn't just a matter of saying, "We're waiting for the Messiah." It was a willingness to sacrifice and consider the Messiah top priority.

Mary and Joseph were willing to begin their married life in a most unconventional way, to be misunderstood, and to flee to Egypt. The shepherds thought that the Messiah was so important that they left their whole flock to visit the baby in the manger. Simeon was "righteous and devout," looking forward to the coming of the Messiah. His seeing Jesus was the crowning point of a lifetime of putting God first. Anna "did not depart from the temple, worshipping with fasting and prayer night and day." Her number-one concern was God and His plan for the world.

Think of the courage and dedication of the wise men. They must have had to put up with the displeasure and ridicule of friends and family members whose adjectives for them never included the word "wise." Such a long journey must have cost a lot of money. It certainly meant leaving business and family responsibilities. It must have been terribly tiring (just try riding a camel for a few weeks!). Imagine their disappointment, and renewed determination, when they found no baby king at Jerusalem! All of these who experienced the first Christmas paid a price, but it was well worth it.

It is no different today. The spiritual principle remains the same. The birth of Jesus takes place again in the lives of those who seek for Him with all their hearts. If you seek the beauty and blessing of the Christ-child, you will find Him. But if you're all wrapped up in decorating, cooking, eating, buying presents and partying, you're certain to miss Christmas.

"Now there was a man in Jerusalem, whose name was Simeon, and this man was righteous and devout, looking for the consolation of Israel, and the Holy Spirit was upon him. And it had been revealed to him by the Holy Spirit that he should not see death before he had seen the Lord's Christ. And inspired by the Spirit he came into the temple; and when the parents brought in the child Jesus, to do for him according to the custom of the law, he took him up in his arms and blessed God and said, 'Lord, now lettest thou thy servant depart in peace, according to thy word; for mine eyes have seen thy salvation' " (Luke 2:25-30).

1. How do you think Simeon got so close to God?
2. Why didn't Simeon miss Christmas?
3. Are there actions or attitudes in your life which are causing you to miss, not only Christmas, but many of God's other blessings as well?

Week Seven

THE ONE AND ONLY JESUS

Jesus Is Not a "Once Upon a Time" Person

How would you react to a newspaper article which stated that John F. Kennedy had never been assassinated, that he is hiding out on a Caribbean Island, and that he healed many people while he was president? Certainly, the reading public, gullible though they may be, would ask a lot of questions and investigate the matter. They could interview all the members of the Kennedy family, people who worked at the White House, and those who witnessed the shooting in Dallas that fateful day—not to mention the mortician. It's just not possible to make a person into a legend just by writing a few things about him or her.

It takes centuries for a legend to develop, and even then historians do their best to rid people of their cherished tales, such as the one about George Washington and the cherry tree. They also go out of their way to assure us that the father of our country was no saint and on occasion displayed a fierce temper.

Some people have theorized that Jesus was a very good person but that the New Testament account of Him is mostly legend. However, the time lapse between the crucifixion of Jesus and the writing of the New Testament was not long enough to allow a legend to develop. F. F. Bruce, a noted biblical scholar, believes that Galatians was written in A.D. 48, just eighteen years after the crucifixion of Christ. He also claims that 1 and 2 Thessalonians, Philippians, 1 and 2 Corinthians, and Romans were all written before A.D. 60. He goes on to say, "In this country a majority of modern scholars fix the dates of the four Gospels as follows: Matthew 85-90 (A.D.), Mark 65 (A.D.), Luke 80-85 (A.D.), John 90-100 (A.D.). I should be inclined to date the first three Gospels rather earlier; Mark shortly after A.D. 60, Luke between 60 and 70, and Matthew shortly after A.D. 70."[1]

Dr. William F. Albright, a world famous archeologist, said that there was no reason to believe that any of the Gospels was written later than A.D. 70.[2] Early church leaders (called the Apostolic Fathers), "writing mostly between A.D. 90 and 160, give indication of familiarity with most of the books of the New Testament."[3]

New Testament readers were in a good position to check up on the facts. When I visited the Holy Land, I was surprised to see how small Old Jerusalem really was. The "little town of Bethlehem" really is little. So is Nazareth. In small towns news travels fast and everybody knows what happens there.

It wouldn't have been hard to ask the people who knew Jesus

whether the things written about Him were true. People would have had reason for checking into these things, for belief in Christ meant a break from the established religion and possible persecution from both Jews and Romans. There would be many people willing to discuss it. (Just ask your grandfather about something that happened thirty or forty years ago and you'll see what I mean.) First-century Christians had a lot at stake. They had to make sure the Jesus they believed in was for real.

But you, too, have reasons for making certain what kind of a person Jesus is. Intellectually, you may have always believed that Jesus is real. But do you treat Him like a real person? Do you spend time talking to Him, reading His word and enjoying His presence? Or do you act as if He were just a picture on the wall, a once-upon-a-time person?

"For we did not follow cleverly devised myths when we made known to you the power and coming or our Lord Jesus Christ, but we were eyewitnesses of his majesty. For when he received honor and glory from God the Father and the voice was borne to him by the Majestic Glory, 'This is my beloved Son, with whom I am well pleased,' we heard this voice borne from heaven, for we were with him on the holy mountain. And we have the prophetic word made more sure. You will do well to pay attention to this as to a lamp shining in a dark place, until the day dawns and the morning star rises in your hearts" (2 Pet. 1:16-19).

1. What evidence does Peter give for the truth of what he writes about Jesus?
2. Notice that God's Word is a light in a dark place. When it becomes part of you, it's like daylight in your heart. What are you doing to make God's Word the "day" that "dawns" in your heart?
3. Would you pay more attention to the words of Jesus if He came into your bedroom and spoke them to you? Why or why not?

The "Make-Your-Own-Jesus Kit" Is Out of Stock

Can you imagine your history teacher standing up in front of your class saying, "Napoleon was a tall blond football player who

took vacations on an island in the Mediterranean'"? History is the study of *factual* information about the past, not a field day for one's imagination. History, and court evidence today, is based on the assumption that people tell the truth about others, unless they have a reason to lie or are mentally imcompetent.

For a long time people searched for a purely human Jesus whom they wanted to call "the historical Jesus." But, "a purely human Jesus like they sought never existed."[4] Archbishop William Temple says, "It is now recognized that the one Christ for whose existence there is any evidence at all is a miraculous Figure making stupendous claims."[5]

Even ancient historical sources, which tell us barely more than the fact that He existed, present a *supernatural* Jesus. The Roman historian Tacitus (A.D. 55-120) tells us of Jesus' crucifixion. The Jewish Talmud explains that He died "in the evening of passover."[6] Josephus, a Jewish historian of the first century, wrote, "There was about this time, Jesus, a wise man, if it be lawful to call him a man, for he was a doer of wonderful works—a teacher of such men as receive the truth with pleasure. He drew over to him both many of the Jews, and many of the Gentiles. He was [the] Christ; and when Pilate, at the suggestion of the principal men amongst us, had condemned him to the cross, those who loved him at the first did not forsake him, for he appeared to them alive again the third day. . ."[7]

Tertullian, a church leader who lived from about A.D. 155-200, wrote in his defense of Christianity, "Tiberius [emporor under whom Jesus was crucified] accordingly, in whose days the Christian name made its entry into the world, having himself received intelligence from Palestine of events which had clearly shown the truth of Christ's divinity, brought the matter before the senate, with his own decision in favor of Christ. The senate, because it had not given the approval itself, rejected his proposal. Caesar held to his opinion, threatening wrath against all the accusers of the Christians."[8] People have noted that Tertullian would never have mentioned this without having reliable information, for the Romans kept good records and the enemies of Christianity were bound to consult them.

The Jesus of history was no ordinary man. Do you sometimes take out your kit and construct your own nonsupernatural Jesus? One who can't forgive you and your boyfriend? One who can't help you trust people again? Or who can't show you His will for next year? Do you live as though a Jesus who has all power doesn't exist?

"Jesus Christ is the same yesterday and today and for ever" (Heb. 13:8).

"And Jesus came and said to them, 'All authority in heaven and on earth has been given to me' " (Matt. 28:18).

"Jesus Christ, who has gone into heaven and is at the right hand of God, with angels, authorities, and powers subject to him" (1 Pet. 3:21-22).

1. What do you learn about the power and authority of Jesus from these verses?
2. What things in your life frighten you and are too big for you to handle?
3. Why don't you pray about these things and give them to the One who has all authority on heaven and on earth?

No Committees, Please

A wise person once remarked, "A camel is a horse designed by a committee." A committee can be a form of organized confusion. As anyone who has worked on a committee can testify, it is extremely difficult for a group of people to agree on the wording of a report which they must submit as a group. Yet, there are those who would have us believe that the New Testament writers formed a committee to exaggerate the life of Jesus and declare Him to be God. Not likely. The New Testament was written down while people who knew Jesus were still alive and able to refute falsehoods. But there are other good reasons for believing that Jesus was not set up by His press agents.

First of all, if the New Testament writers wanted to invent a Messiah that everyone would follow, they could have done a better job. People wanted a king who would deliver them from Roman rule—not a Jesus who *died* for their sins, rose again and went to heaven. The Jewish people were in no mood to wait until the second coming of Christ. They wanted the prophecies about His kingly power to be fulfilled right away.

Second, the unique personality of Jesus does not "fit" the Jewish mindset. Jean-Jacques Rousseau, a Frenchman whose philosophy directly opposed the teachings of Jesus, said this:

> The facts concerning Socrates, of which no one entertains a doubt, are less attested than those concerning Jesus Christ. . . . It would be more inconceivable that several men should have united to fabricate that book, than that a single person have furnished the subject of it. Jewish authors would never have invented either that style or that morality; and the gospel has marks of truths so great, so striking, so utterly inimitable, that the invention of it would be more astonishing than the hero.[9]

Finally, the New Testament authors were "monotheistic to the core."[10] They had to have very strong evidence before they would admit that Jesus was God. Paul had studied under the most famous rabbi of his time. To worship the man born in Bethlehem and to call Him "Lord" went against everything he had ever been taught. And he did it only after an unnerving vision on the road to Damascus.

It's just too far-fetched to believe that the Jerusalem Press Club would collaborate to make Jesus of Nazareth world famous by declaring Him to be God. Besides, readers wouldn't have believed in the deity of Jesus without evidence.

The evidence of Jesus' deity is found not only in healings and the

resurrection, but in *changed lives*. Paul, who at first wanted to kill Christians, became a fearless apostle. The early Christians, when persecuted by the Romans, amazed their captors with their joy and courage.

It's the same today. Not only can Jesus save and give you eternal life, but He also can keep changing you to make you more like himself. Have you ever thought that He would like to deal with your moodiness and your tendency to get depressed when things don't go your way? If you willingly give up self-pity and obey Jesus at every point, He will change you. But why aren't you giving Him a chance to prove His deity in your life?

"Now the Lord is the Spirit, and where the Spirit of the Lord is, there is freedom. And we all, with unveiled face, beholding the glory of the Lord, are being changed into his likeness from one degree of glory to another; for this comes from the Lord who is Spirit" (2 Cor. 3:17-18).

1. Why is it wrong to say, "I'm just a moody person and I can't do anything to change that"?
2. Are you willing to let the Jesus who proved himself to be God keep changing you?
3. Pray now and ask Jesus where He wants to start changing your life.

True and False Test

Suppose I said, "It's raining outside," or "I am Napoleon," or, "I will save the world." In each case I would be either lying or telling the truth, not something "in between." People today want to get off the hook by using terms such as exaggerate, miscommunicate, and "little white lies"; but the ugly fact remains, that each time a person opens his mouth, he is either lying or telling the truth.

The Jews of Jesus' day recognized this. They realized that if Jesus wasn't telling the truth, He had to be lying. So they attributed His supernatural power to "black magic"—"But the Pharisees said, 'He casts out demons by the prince of demons' " (Matt. 9:34). The miracles of Jesus "are also discussed in the Jewish Talmud. Some Rabbis taught that Christ learned the secret of magic while in Egypt."[11]

The Jews were thoroughly upset by a man who claimed to forgive sins, who accepted the worship of people, and who said such things as, " 'You have heard. . . ," You shall not kill; and whoever kills shall be liable to judgment." But I say to you that everyone who is angry with his brother shall be liable to judgment' " (Matt. 5:21-22). They were unwilling to even entertain the idea that Jesus might be telling the truth. But they did know that if He was lying, Jesus was guilty of blasphemy (speech or action that is mocking or imitating God). And their law read, " 'He who blasphemes the name of the Lord shall be put to death' " (Lev. 24:16). Either they had to believe on Him or they had to kill Him.

They were too logical and too intelligent to say He was a prophet or a great teacher. Great teachers don't boldly assert such things as, " 'I am . . . the truth,'"[12] or, " 'I am the light of the world.' "[13] C. S. Lewis is often quoted, but he still says it best:

"I'm ready to accept Jesus as a great moral teacher, but I don't accept His claim to be God." That is the one thing we must not say. A man who was merely a man and said the sort of things Jesus said would not be a great moral teacher. He would either be a lunatic—on a level with a man who says he is a poached egg—or else he would be the Devil of Hell. You must make your choice. Either this man was and is the Son of God; or else a madman or something worse. You can shut Him up for a fool, you can spit on Him and kill Him as a demon; or you can fall at His feet and call Him Lord and God. But let us not come up with any patronizing nonsense about His being a great human teacher. He has not left that open to us. He did not intend to.[14]

Do you fall at Jesus' feet and call Him Lord, or do you treat Him as a co-philosopher whose ideas about life are *almost* as good as yours? Do you treat His command, " 'Judge not, that you be not judged,' " as truth, or do you get a couple of friends as your defense lawyers to explain to Jesus your position while you criticize your parents, your teachers and your church? What Jesus said is either true or false. "None of the above" is not one of the choices.

" *'Judge not, that you be not judged. For with the judgment you pronounce you will be judged, and the measure you give will be the measure you get. Why do you see the speck that is in your brother's eye, but do not notice the log that is in your own eye? Or how can you say to your brother, "Let me take the speck out of your eye," when there is a log in your own eye? You hypocrite, first take the log out of your own eye, and then you will see clearly to take the speck out of your brother's eye'* " (Matt. 7:1-5).

1. What do these verses say about your complaints that Miss Jones is the worst teacher that anyone could have?
2. Why is it easier to excuse faults in *yourself* than in others?
3. Have you ever asked Jesus to show you the log in your eye?
4. After you get the log out of your eye, pray and ask Jesus what attitude He wants you to take toward Miss Jones' typing class.

Was Jesus Merely Out of His Mind?

The evening newscaster reports on a man who attracted great crowds of people. He gave a speech last night in which he had said such things as, "Before Abraham was, I am," "Because I tell the truth, you do not believe me. Which of you convicts me of sin!" and "If God were your Father, you would love me, for I proceeded and came forth from God; I came not of my own accord, but he sent me. You are of your father the devil."[15]

Your first thought might be that this orator belongs in a psych ward. And If you found out that in his next speech he stated, "He who loves father or mother more than me is not worthy of me; and he who loves son or daughter more than me is not worthy of me,[16] you would be more convinced that the man was nuts.

Yet, Jesus really said *all* those things. And He was misunderstood. His family, for instance, was worried about His spending too much time with the crowds and not getting his rest: "Then he went home; and the crowd came together again, so that they could not even eat. And when his friends heard it, they went out to seize him, for they said, 'He is beside himself' " (Mark 3:19-21). But that was before Jesus fed the five thousand and raised Lazarus from the dead. Later, these people changed their minds. In fact, James, a half brother of Jesus, became a leader of the church in Jerusalem and a martyr for Jesus Christ.

Jesus displayed none of the indecision and desire to escape reality usually observed in the mentally ill. The poise Jesus showed under the pressure of trial and crucifixion is remarkable for even a sane person. He was never frustrated, never in a hurry, and never too concerned about His own problems to help others. His sleeping through a dreadful storm proves that He was not subject to insomnia. His teachings show balance, profound insight, and beauty that are unmatched.

C. S. Lewis observes "The discrepancy between depth and sanity . . . of His moral teaching and the rampant megalomania [thinking of oneself as someone great] which must lie behind His theological teaching unless He is indeed God has never been satisfactorily explained."[17]

Of course if Jesus is divine, He could logically and truthfully make every one of those statements. And that is just the point. If Jesus is God, He has a right to demand all your love.

"And Jesus said to them, 'Follow me and I will make you become fishers of men.' And immediately they left their nets and followed him. And going on a little farther, he saw James the sons of Zebedee and John his brother, who were in their boat mending the nets. And immediately he called them; and they left their father Zebedee in the boat with the hired servants, and followed him" (Mark 1:17-20).

"When they had finished breakfast, Jesus said to Simon Peter, 'Simon, son of John, do you love me more than these?' He said to him, 'Yes, Lord; you know that I love you.' He said to him, 'Feed my lambs' " (John 21:15).

1. What had Peter already done to prove that he loved Jesus?
2. What further commitment was Jesus demanding of Peter?
3. What is the test of *your* love for Jesus at this time in your life?
4. Are you willing to love Jesus more than your boyfriend or girlfriend?

Miracles, or Hocus-Pocus?

In each of the Gospels much space is devoted to the miracles of Jesus. The gospel writers were willing to give their lives for the messages they preached about Jesus and part of that message was the miracles performed by Jesus. Their accounts include details such as names of people, places, and the number of people fed with five loaves and two fish. Such facts could easily be double-checked by skeptical readers. There are testimonies outside the Scriptures which verify Jesus' miracles. Even Celsus, an anti-Christian philosopher who lived in the second century, mentions them. They are also discussed in the Jewish Talmud.[18] It has been noted that writing a biography of Jesus without mentioning miracles is like composing a life of Napoleon without reference to a single battle.

No one can explain away the Jesus who could calm the sea, raise the dead and heal leprosy. But His perfect life was even more significant than His miracles. Both the Old and New Testament teach us that miracles can be performed by the power of the devil. The Pharisees knew this and tried to accuse Jesus of using Satan's power. It just didn't stick. People saw in His life a moral miracle greater than His healings.

Jesus considered His words to be more important than His miracles. His miracles were simply signs that those who would not listen to Him had to deal with. He said, " 'The words that I say to you I do not speak on my own authority,' " but added " 'Believe me that I am in the Father and the Father in me; or else believe me for the sake of the works themselves' " (John 14:10).

Above all, the miracles of Jesus taught spiritual truths and provided object lessons that confirmed His words. He didn't turn water into wine just to save the bridegroom the embarrassment of running out of wine. The stone jugs had been filled with water to be used in the Jewish ritual of purification. Jesus turned that water into wine to signify that His glorious gospel would supersede the law of Moses. His first miracle showed people that He was the Messiah who had come to initiate a new era. When he fed the five thousand with real bread and real fish, Jesus was saying, "I am the bread of life," the one who can satisfy the hunger in each human heart. When He healed the blind man, He was showing himself as the "Light of the World" who could also open the eyes of the spiritually blind.

Jesus has not changed. He still works miracles and He still works them with a spiritual purpose in mind. Jesus' *life* was more important than His miracles. And the quality of the life that you lead is more important than the miracles God leads you to pray for.

"And if I have all faith, so as to remove mountains, but have not love, I am nothing" (1 Cor. 13:2).

" *'Truly, truly, I say to you, he who believes in me will also do the works that I do; and greater works than these will he do, because I go to the Father' "* (John 14:12).

1. Of what value is great faith without love and holiness?
2. Because faith without love is worthless, should we forget about faith? Why not?
3. Which area of your life yells "Hypocrite!" every time your faith gets fired up to do great things for God?

Not in the Same Category

A junior high student said it in a contest speech she was giving on social problems: "And we should all follow the teachings of great religious leaders like Jesus, Buddha and Mohammed."

The tendency to put all the founders of the world's great religions in the same category is very common. But does it make sense? Consider the facts and you'll see that there are several things which set Jesus apart from all the others.

Jesus always knew *who* He was, *why* He was sent, and *what* His message was. At age twelve He was instructing the Jewish leaders and telling Mary and Joseph, " 'I must be in my Father's house.' "[19] Buddha, according to tradition, spent six years "living on one sesamum seed or one grain of rice"[20] a day until finally one night under the bo-tree he determined the cause and cure of evil. Mohammed spent hours and hours alone in a cave in the desert; there he received his ideas through visions which continued for twelve years. Confucius hoped to improve his character if only he could have had fifty more years to study.

Jesus claimed He *was* the truth; the others only claimed to *teach* it. Jesus said, "Follow me"; the others only asked people to follow their teachings. Confucius claimed to be only a "transmitter, not an originator"[21] of truth. In Buddha's Eightfold Path (right views, right aims, right speech, right actions, right livelihood, right effort, right mindfulness, and right contemplation), he mentions neither God nor himself. Mohammed taught his understanding of God.

The greatest thing that set Jesus apart from the other religious leaders was His claim to be God (which He proved by His miracles and resurrection). Robert Hume says about Buddha, "He did not teach a personal deity, worship, or prayer. . . . [Eventually] Buddha himself was deified; numerous other deities have been believed in by the majority of Buddhists."[22] Buddha died at age eighty.

Mohammed only claimed to be a prophet. His love of fighting and his problems with his eleven wives would not lead one to believe in his divinity. He shocked his followers by dying. He left no son or successor, which proved to be a real problem for Moslems.

Confucius avoided teaching on the supernatural. He taught history, poetry, literature, proprieties (good manners), government, natural science, and music. He candidly confessed his moral shortcomings, including drinking too much. After Confucius' death, his tomb became very important. In 195 B.C. the Emperor of China offered animal sacrifices there.

As you can see, Jesus just isn't in the same category as other founders of world religions. His claims are unique and they make people feel uncomfortable. Go ahead and mix and match ideas from all *other* religions, taking an idea here and disregarding one there. But let the message and person of Jesus stand alone as the only standard of truth. If Jesus contradicts a statement, whether it be from your psychology text, the President of the United States, or your best friend, you must believe Jesus and disregard the other.

"Jesus then said to the Jews who believed in him, 'If you will continue in my word, you are truly my disciples, and you will know the truth and the truth will make you free'" (John 8:31, 32).

1. What things does Jesus claim for the words He speaks?
2. Can you give some examples of how believing the wrong thing can put people in bondage? Do you have enough faith in Jesus to believe His Word is *always* true, and to stake your life on it?
3. Is there a "test issue" in your life? Whom are you going to believe, Jesus or someone else?

Week Eight

JESUS SAID *THAT?*

But, Jesus Didn't Say He Was God

It is likely that Queen Elizabeth II has never said these exact words: "I am the Queen of England." She doesn't need to say them. She just goes around acting like the Queen of England. She opens Parliament, she represents her country on state visits and at times, she wears a crown.

You won't find any record of Jesus saying, "I am God." But He did *act* like God. And He claimed the right to do things that only God can do, such as the ability to forgive sins.

When Jesus was speaking in a private home to an overflow crowd, friends of a paralyzed man removed tiles from the roof and lowered their friend on a cot just in front of the place where Jesus was standing.

Jesus said to that sick man, " 'My son, your sins are forgiven.' " Onlookers questioned this because their theology was correct. They wondered, " 'Why does this man speak thus? It is blasphemy! Who can forgive sins but God alone?' " Jesus knew exactly what they were thinking, so He asked them a question. " 'Which is easier, to say to the paralytic, "Your sins are forgiven," or to say, "Rise, take up your pallet and walk?" But that you may know that the Son of man has authority on earth to forgive sins'—he said to the paralytic—'I say to you, rise, take up your pallet and go home.' And he rose, and immediately took up the pallet and went out before them all" (Mark 2:5, 7, 9-12).

While Jesus was eating at a dinner party, a woman of the streets came and wet His feet with her tears, wiped them with her hair, and poured expensive perfume on them. Those who knew this woman's bad reputation informed Jesus about this sinful person. Jesus, however, explained that those who are forgiven of more, love more. Then He said, " 'Therefore I tell you, her sins, which are many, are forgiven, for she loved much; but he who is forgiven little, loves little,' and he said to her, 'Your sins are forgiven' " (Luke 7:47-48).

One person telling another that he is forgiven of *all* his sins makes no sense. One can only forgive sins committed against *himself*. But since all sins are committed against God, He can forgive a person of all his or her sins. This is exactly what Jesus claimed to do, and He healed the paralytic in order to prove that His claim was not mere words.

The people in these biblical accounts accepted the forgiveness of Jesus. Will you? Of course you have a guilt complex. You're guilty, aren't you? But if you admit your wrongdoing and your wrong thinking, and accept Jesus' pardon, He will set you free. Jesus is God and He wants to prove it to you.

"In him we have redemption through his blood, the forgiveness of our trespasses, according to the riches of his grace which he lavished upon us" (Eph. 1:7-8).

"My little children, I am writing this to you so that you may not sin; but if any one does sin, we have an advocate [one who pleads our case] with the Father, Jesus Christ the righteous; and he is the expiation [sacrifice] for our sins, and not for ours only but also for the sins of the whole world" (1 John 2:1-2).

1. Which statements in the above verses show us that Jesus wants to forgive us?
2. Why is it unnecessary to run around feeling guilty all the time?
3. Do you have some sin that needs to be confessed so Jesus can set you free from your guilt?

$Y = 2X - 3$

In grade school you learned that three plus three is the same as two plus four. In algebra the principle holds true in an equation such as $y = 2x - 3$. In geometry, the whole that is equal to the sum of its parts may be made up of different sized parts. Although no analogy is adequate, this might give you some insight into the fact that Jesus of Nazareth, who healed the sick, preached the Sermon on the Mount, and rose from the dead, is equal to the invisible God.

Jesus often used the "I equal God" equation in His teaching. When Philip said to Him, " 'Lord, show us the Father, and we shall be satisfied,' " Jesus answered, " 'Have I been with you so long, and yet you do not know me, Philip? He who has seen me has seen the Father' " (John 14:8-9). Jesus told the Pharisees, " 'If you knew me, you would know my Father also' " (John 8:19). Later He proclaimed, " 'He who sees me sees him who sent me' " (John 12:45). Jesus taught clearly that to know Him is to know God and to see Him is to see God.

Jesus also taught that to believe on Him is to believe on God. He said, " 'He who believes in me, believes not in me but in him who sent me' " (John 12:44); " 'This is the work of God, that you believe in him whom he has sent' " (John 6:29); and " 'Believe in God, believe also in me' " (John 14:1).

Jesus equated people's attitudes toward Him with their attitudes toward God. " 'Whoever receives me, receives not me but him who sent me' " (Mark 9:37); " 'He who hates me hates my Father also' " (John 15:23); and " 'He who does not honor the Son does not honor the Father who sent him' " (John 5:23).[1]

You may be convinced that Jesus is God, but still you may not be honoring Him. Does your high regard for Jesus influence the way you live? You no doubt put your best foot forward when you are around people you consider to be important. Is Jesus that important to you? Do you keep in mind He hears every word you say to your mother? He even knows your every thought. He notices the attitudes with which you clear the table or shovel the snow. He knows what you really think of Him.

Are you willing to honor Jesus in the locker room and in biology class? Or are the opinions of your peers more important to you than the opinion of Jesus? His words still hold true. If you don't honor Jesus, you don't honor God.

" *'Well did Isaiah prophesy of you, when he said: "This people honors me with their lips, but their heart is far from me"' "*
(Matt. 15:7-8).

"So every one who acknowledges me before men, I also will acknowledge before my Father who is in heaven; but whoever denies me before men, I also will deny before my Father who is in heaven"
(Matt. 10:32-33).

1. What does it mean to *honor* Jesus?
2. Why is Jesus worthy of your honor?
3. Are there any people whose opinions mean more to you than the opinion of Jesus?
4. You may not be very brave. Yet, if you obey Jesus by honoring Him, He'll give you the strength. Ask Him for that right now.

Judgment Day and Every Day

Imagine attending church in a small resort town with your family and hearing the pastor say, "You won't go to heaven unless you do exactly as *I* say." You would be horrified if he continued, "I'm coming back at the end of time to judge each one of you according to your obedience to me." No one needs to tell you that only God has the right to judge His creatures. Yet, Jesus claimed He had that prerogative.

Jesus said, " 'On that day many will say to me, "Lord, Lord, did we not prophesy in your name, and cast out demons in your name, and do many mighty works in your name?" And then I will declare to them, "I never knew you; depart from me, you evildoers' " (Matt. 7:22-23).

In another sermon His listeners heard, " 'For as the Father has life in himself, so he has granted the Son also to have life in himself, and has given him authority to execute judgment, because he is the Son of man. Do not marvel at this; for the hour is coming when all who are in the tombs will hear his voice and come forth, those who have done good, to the resurrection of life, and those who have done evil, to the resurrection of judgment' " (John 5:26-27). That is quite a claim. If Jesus had been running around in a souped-up chariot with mag wheels, 12-inch racing slicks, and signs in five languages reading "I AM GOD," the message would not have been clearer than that of this statement.

Jesus further declared, "He who rejects me and does not receive my sayings has a judge; the word that I have spoken will be his judge on the last day' " (John 12:48). Think of it! On judgment day your life will be measured against every word that was spoken by Jesus, including, "Love your enemies," " 'Let your light so shine before men,' " and " 'Do not be anxious about your life.' "[2]

The thought of being judged by these words is frightening, but Jesus has sent the Holy Spirit to enable you to live up to His commands. If you are fully committed to obeying Jesus, the Holy Spirit, whom Jesus promised would " 'guide you into all truth,' "[3] will teach you how to love the girl who is spreading lies about you, how to witness to your friends at school, and how to stop worrying about how you look. Obeying the commands of Jesus will help you on judgment day—and every day.

" 'When the Son of man comes in his glory, and all the angels with him, then he will sit on his glorious throne. Before him will be gathered all the nations, and he will separate them one from another as a shepherd separates the sheep from the goats, and he will place the sheep at his right hand, "Come, . . . inherit the kingdom prepared for you . . . ; for I was hungry and you gave me food, I was thirsty and you gave me drink, I was a stranger and you welcomed me, I was naked and you clothed me, I was sick and you visited me, I was in prison and you came to me. . . ; 'Truly, I say to you, as you

did it to one of the least of these my brethren, you did it to me" ' "
(Matt. 25:31-36, 40).

1. Why should this passage erase any doubt in your mind that Jesus claimed to be God?
2. What is the difference between a do-gooder and a person who does God's will under the direction of the Holy Spirit?
3. If Jesus truly is God, what *specific* change needs to be made in your life *today*?

Needles, Camels, Houses and Land

What if you suddenly became a multi-millionaire? Would you enjoy deciding what to spend your money on? You'd probably be very involved with your mansion, your lake home, your cars, your expensive clothes and your vacations. What if someone asked you to sell it all, to contribute every penny to the poor, and become his slave? Would it be hard to turn him down?

You'd probably say, "Forget it," without thinking twice. You'd also recognize that no person could rightly ask you to do such a thing.

But Jesus does have the right. A very rich young man asked Him an important question: " 'Teacher, what must I do, to have eternal life?' " Jesus answered, " 'If you would be perfect, go, sell what you possess and give to the poor, and you will have treasure in heaven; and come, follow me.' "

The young man knew that Jesus was filled with the goodness of God, that He was the " 'One there is who is good.' " Jesus as God had the right to tell him what to do. But he turned away, not with disgust toward another for meddling in his affairs, but with sorrow. He had refused God because he loved his possessions too much. The stakes were high; eternal life was in the balance. He knew it, but he blew it.

Jesus then commented that it is easier for a camel to go through the eye of a needle than for a rich man to enter the kingdom of heaven. This reminded the disciples of what they had left to follow Jesus. Peter, Andrew, James and John had left their fishing nets. Matthew had quit his job as a tax collector.

Peter observed, " 'Lo, we have left everything and followed

you.' " He asked then, " 'What then shall we have?' "

Jesus gave him an answer that no one but God could have given. " 'Truly, I say to you, in the new world, when the Son of man shall sit on his glorious throne, you who have followed me will also sit on twelve thrones, judging the twelve tribes of Israel. And everyone who has left houses or brothers or sisters or father or mother or children or lands, for my name's sake, will receive a hundredfold, and inherit eternal life" (Matt. 19:16-29).

If Jesus is not the real owner of your possessions, something is wrong. If Jesus owns your car, you will use it to give rides to others, even when inconvenient for you. You won't get all upset over the spot on the dress that belongs to Jesus!

You may not have any houses or land to leave for Jesus, but He may be asking you to share your clothes with your sister or to lend your skis to your little brother. And you may need God's special grace, even to get this little camel through the eye of the needle.

"And Jesus said to his disciples, 'Truly, I say to you, it will be hard for a rich man to enter the kingdom of heaven. Again I tell you, it is easier for a camel to go through the eye of a needle than for a rich man to enter the kingdom of God.' When the disciples heard this they were greatly astonished, saying, 'Who then can be saved?' But Jesus looked at them and said to them, 'With men this is impossible, but with God all things are possible' " (Matt. 19:23-26).

" 'Do not lay up for yourselves treasures on earth, where moth and rust consume and where thieves break in and steal, but lay up for yourselves treasures in heaven, where neither moth nor rust consumes and where thieves do not break in and steal. For where your treasure is, there will your heart be also' " (Matt. 6:19-21).

1. In what way is God asking you to give Him one of your earthly possessions?
2. Do you have any treasure in heaven? If not, what can you begin doing about it?

Humble Harry Strikes Again

The "I-can't-play-the-piano-very-well" humility from a concert pianist is sickening. The Humble Harry who keeps repeating, "Oh, I never do anything right," is both a liar and a mailbox for compliments.

Jesus is the example of true humility. His formula was *truth plus complete self-sacrifice.* Jesus couldn't honestly say "humble" things about himself. They wouldn't have been true. The Apostle Paul declared, "I am the foremost of sinners,"[4] but Jesus asked, " 'Which of you convicts me of sin?' "[5] No one accused Him of wrongdoing. Jesus told His disciples how fortunate they were to have Him around: " 'Truly, I say to you, many prophets and righteous men longed to see what you see, and did not see it, and to hear what you hear, and did not hear it' " (Matt. 13:17). He also said such things as, " 'The queen of the South will arise at the judgment with the men of this generation and condemn them; for she came from the ends of the earth to hear the wisdom of Solomon, and behold, something greater than Solomon is here' " (Luke 11:31), and, " 'For you always have the poor with you, but you will not always have me' " (Matt. 26:11). These are honest statements from the Son of God.

Yet, Jesus was never a show-off. He never performed a stunt miracle. He always put the welfare of others before His own. He left the glories of heaven and took on human form. He talked to the Samaritan woman at the well even though He was exhausted and may have preferred solitude. He took time to bless the children and He washed the disciples' feet. He willingly died for the world and cared for the thief dying next to Him. His best friends left Him in the lurch and even Peter pretended he didn't know Him. No one ever made a greater sacrifice for others than Jesus did.

We need to let Jesus show us what true humility is. It isn't being Milk-toast Matilda or Humble Harry. Of course, we can't make claims like Jesus made because we aren't God. But we should never say something false in order to appear humble. Paul, in Ephesians 4:15, defines humility in speech as, "speaking the truth in love."

Humility sometimes means keeping your mouth shut even though you know all the right answers. It means doing the dishes with a smile or offering to work on homecoming night so your friend can go to the game. It means being willing to get a lower grade on the chemistry test by using your study time to visit a sick neighbor. It means graciously admitting that you are wrong. It means telling the truth and putting your rights last.

"Jesus, knowing that the Father had given all things into his hands, and that he had come from God and was going to God, rose from supper, laid aside his garments, and girded himself with a towel. Then he poured water into a basin, and began to wash the disciples' feet, and to wipe them with the towel with which he was girded. When he had washed their feet, and taken his garments, and resumed his place, he said to them, 'Do you know what I have done to you? You call me Teacher and Lord; and you are right, for so I am. If I then, your Lord and Teacher, have washed your feet, you also ought to wash one another's feet' " (John 13:3-5, 12-14).

1. Have you ever tried to be humble by saying things that were not true?
2. What are the dirty jobs you hate to do? Have you ever volunteered for these so someone else wouldn't have to?
3. Is your pride keeping you from obeying God in some way? Pray about this.

The Life That's Worth Living

The couple with a new baby, the man who has just been told he has cancer, and the girl who has just found out that her boyfriend was critically injured in a motorcycle accident have been reminded that life comes from God. Life is very precious and very fragile.

But as amazing and glorious as *physical* life is, it can never compare with *eternal* life. Just think of it—a beautiful, fulfilling and joyous life forever and ever. Certainly no one but God could give anybody eternal life.

Jesus claimed not only to give physical life and eternal life, but He claimed to *be* life itself. The first chapter of John says of Jesus, "All things were made through him, and without him was not anything made that was made. In him was life, and the life was the light of men."[6]

Jesus told His friend Martha, who was mourning the loss of her brother, Lazarus, " 'I am the resurrection and the life; he who believes in me, though he die, yet shall he live' " (John 11:25). And to prove it, He raised Lazarus from the dead.

Life and death are beyond the control of the ordinary mortal, but Jesus was in control of both His death and His resurrection—" 'I lay down my life, that I may take it again. No one takes it from me, but I lay it down of my own accord. I have power to lay it down, and I have power to take it again' " (John 10:17, 18).

Jesus also claimed to *give* eternal life to people. He declared, " 'I give them eternal life, and they shall never perish, and no one shall snatch them out of my hand' " (John 10:28). Before His crucifixion Jesus prayed, " 'Father, the hour has come; glorify thy Son that the Son may glorify thee, since thou hast given him power over all flesh, to give eternal life to all whom thou hast given him' " (John 17:1, 2).

Jesus also said, " 'I came that they may have life, and have it abundantly' " (John 10:10). People rebel against existence without meaning. Jesus came to fill your lives with every good thing. His love for us never runs out. He offers peace, joy and purpose—but all these gifts must be accepted on *His* terms.

Jesus wants to give *you* the life that is worth living.

"Jesus said to them, 'I am the bread of life; he who comes to me shall not hunger, and he who believes in me shall never thirst' " (John 6:35).

" 'Every one who drinks of this water will thirst again, but whoever drinks of the water that I shall give him will never thirst;

*the water that I shall give him will become in him a spring of water
welling up to eternal life'* " (John 4:13-14).

1. In what ways can Jesus be the "bread of life" and "living water"
   to you?
2. Is it possible to trust Jesus completely and to be depressed at the
   same time?
3. What things make you turn off the "faucet" which has a never-
   ending supply of the living water of Jesus?

The Truth About Worry

The I Always Tell the Truth Club is pretty hard to join. For one
thing, it's not always to our advantage to tell the truth. A Sunday
school teacher, as the story goes, got this definition of a lie from a
little boy: A lie is a terrible sin but a very present help in time of
trouble. It often seems easier to bail ourselves out by stretching the
truth in some way. Even if we are sincere, our faulty memories, incorrect information, or prejudice often keep us from telling the
truth.

Jesus, however, claimed to always speak the truth. He said, " 'I
am the . . . truth' " (John 14:6).

If you listen to great orators or read famous books, you'll find
that an authority in a specific field is often quoted to prove a point.
Jesus, however, was His own authority. He boldly began His sermons with, " 'Truly, truly, *I* say to you. . . .' "[7] He claimed to receive His messages directly from God His Father. "It seems to me,"
or, "in my opinion," were not part of His vocabulary. He never hesi-
tated or revised what He said.

The people who heard Him recognized the authority with which
He spoke. They were amazed and asked, " 'How is it that this man
has learning, when he has never studied?' " (John 7:15). When
Jesus finished speaking, "the crowds were astonished at his teaching, for he taught them as one who had authority, and not as their
scribes" (Matt. 7:28-29).

Jesus even said, " 'Heaven and earth will pass away, but my
words will not pass away' " (Matt. 24:35). By predicting the future
with certainty and giving commands such as, " 'Do not be anxious
about tomorrow,' " and " 'Do not lay up for yourselves treasures
on earth,' "[8] He declared himself to be the absolute standard for
truth. Here's the problem. If what Jesus said is true, you'll have to

change the way you live! You can no longer rationalize greed, self-ishness, or even worry. If you're going to conquer worry, you first must confess it as *sin*, because Jesus *commands* you not to do it and because worry is a slap in the face to the God who takes such good care of you. The second step is to trust the Holy Spirit for a faith-filled response in each situation. The God who can send a blizzard bad enough to close down your city, and who brings spring every year, certainly can protect you from the teacher who has it in for you, and can show you what to do this summer. The Son of God who has all power and all knowledge told us the truth about worry. He commanded you to not worry.

" 'Therefore I tell you, do not be anxious about your life, what you shall eat or what you shall drink, nor about your body, what you shall put on. Is not life more than food, and the body more than clothing? Look at the birds of the air; they neither sow nor reap nor gather into barns, and yet your heavenly Father feeds them. Are you not of more value than they? And which of you by being anxious can add one cubit to his span of life? And why are you anxious about clothing? Consider the lilies of the field, how they grow; they neither toil nor spin; yet I tell you, even Solomon in all his glory was not arrayed like one of these' " (Matt. 6:25-29).

1. What can we learn from birds and lilies?
2. What things are you worrying about instead of trusting Jesus?
3. Ask for forgiveness for your worrying and for faith to put every-thing into God's hands. Then ask the Holy Spirit for wisdom and guidance for your next step.

Week Nine

NOBODY'S PERFECT—EXCEPT JESUS

The Perfect Person Inside You

Could you live and work very closely with someone for three solid years and conclude that he or she had no sin? It's happened only once in history. The disciples of Jesus, who had shared the crowded quarters of a small boat with Him, had seen Him exhausted after a day among large crowds, and had listened to Him talk with angry Pharisees were the ones who claimed He was sinless. They had done virtually everything with Jesus, so they knew Jesus well enough to form a valid opinion. When *they* were in the limelight, there were many tense moments. Even though they were godly men, the disciples argued about who would be the greatest. And they all deserted Jesus just before His trial. The contrast between their behavior and that of Jesus convinced them that Jesus had no sin.

The idea of a perfect, sinless life did not exist in Greek or Roman thought. You have only to read some of their mythology to be convinced of this. And the men who claimed Jesus was sinless were Jews who had been taught since childhood that *all* men are sinners. They were very familiar with verses such as, "The Lord looks down from heaven upon the children of men, to see if there are any that act wisely, that seek after God. They have all gone astray, they are all alike corrupt; there is none that does good, no, not one" (Ps. 14:2-3).

It was no light thing for the apostles to say Jesus was sinless.

Statements are more apt to be true if they are mentioned incidentally than if they concern the main argument the person is presenting. I once realized I was sitting beside an extremely wealthy woman on the train, not because she *tried* to prove that she was rich, but because she casually mentioned the $300 tablecloths she had "picked up" as gifts for her friends and the mink stole she had in her trunk.

The statements the disciples made about Jesus' perfection were not part of a "Jesus is perfect" report. "Their remarks are asides. They are discussing some other subject, and add almost as a parenthesis a reference to His sinlessless."[1]

Although our humanness causes us to make many errors in judgment (we will always spill the Coke, forget to turn off the car lights, or make the awkward comment), God wants to put inside us the character of Jesus. In 1 John 2:6 we are told, "He who says he abides in him ought to walk in the same way in which he walked."

Are you letting the Jesus inside you show through, or are you preventing this by your selfishness, greed and laziness?

"Christ also suffered for you, leaving you an example, that you should follow in his steps. He committed no sin; no guile [deceit] was found on his lips" (1 Peter 2:21-22).

"You know that he appeared to take away sins, and in him there is no sin" (1 John 3:5).

"Jesus, the Son of God, . . . who in every respect has been tempted as we are, yet without sinning" (Heb. 4:14-15).

"For your sake he made him to be sin who knew no sin, so that in him we might become the righteousness of God" (2 Cor. 5:21).

1. List all the things you learn about the character of Jesus from the above verses.
2. What do these verses teach you about God's will for your life?
3. Do you really want the character of Christ, or would you rather keep all your bad habits and cover them up with, "Well, I'm only human"?

If Your Best Friend Doesn't Tell You, Your Enemies Might

We get some interesting insight into the character of Jesus from the accusations made by His enemies. They tried to trap Him many times, but they were unable to build a case against Him.

Jesus was a friend of sinful people and that, in the eyes of the high and mighty Pharisees, was dreadful. He ate with men who collected the taxes for the hated Roman Empire. He was a close friend to those who did not possess spotless reputations. He even allowed a prostitute to pour a bottle of perfume on His feet. The Pharisees argued that a good person would choose a better caliber of friends. But Jesus brought these sinful people up to His level and never condescended to theirs. Matthew, a tax collector, became an apostle, and Mary Magdalene, a prostitute, was the first person to proclaim the resurrection.

The Pharisees then complained that, instead of fasting, Jesus was enjoying the dinner parties He attended. They tried to smear His reputation: " 'Behold, a glutton and a drunkard, a friend of tax collectors and sinners!' " (Matt. 11:19).

They also accused Him of breaking the Sabbath because He healed people and because He once picked a handful of grain and threshed it out in His hands on that day (an act equal to peeling a banana on Sunday). The Pharisees seemed to forget that God had commanded them to keep the Sabbath *holy*, but had not prescribed complete bed rest for the entire nation. They had invented rules which made it illegal to tie a knot, write two letters, go outside wearing a false tooth, or pull out a hair on the Sabbath. These rules did not come from Scripture. It is no wonder that Jesus disagreed with the Pharisees on how to spend the Sabbath.

The beauty of Jesus' life was its *balance*. In spite of His purity, He had great compassion for the worst of sinners. He didn't care for them by long distance, but in a real and human way. Although He was very serious and devout, He showed us by example how to enjoy the good things that God gives in life. He got at the heart of God's commandments and discarded the legalistic baloney.

The Pharisees also charged Jesus with blasphemy (speech or action which mocks or imitates God) because He claimed to forgive sin. At His trial, Jesus admitted that He was the Christ, the Son of God, and that He would be seated at the right hand of God, " 'coming with the clouds of heaven.' "[2] He was again accused of blasphemy. But because He was divine, He had every right to forgive sins and declare that He was the Messiah, the Savior whom God had promised to send to the world.

Jesus' enemies had to hire false witnesses at His trial who accused Jesus of saying, " ' "I will destroy this temple that is made with hands, and in three days I will build another, not made with hands" ' " (Mark 14:58). He actually had said, " 'Destroy this temple [meaning his body], and in three days I will raise it up' " (John 2:19). The false witnesses couldn't agree, Herod wouldn't condemn Him, and Pilate declared Jesus innocent as he washed his hands before the mob. The dying thief said, " 'This man has done nothing wrong,' " and the Roman centurion, who stood by the cross, exclaimed, " 'Truly this was the Son of God.' "[3] It was very hard to find something bad to say about Jesus.

For those of us who follow Jesus, the challenge always remains—to so live that those who are looking for our faults will have a hard time finding them. It's good to make sure that your enemies have no ammunition.

"Maintain good conduct among the Gentiles, so that in case they speak against you as wrongdoers, they may see your good deeds and glorify God on the day of visitation" (1 Pet. 2:12).

"Keep your conscience clear, so that, when you are abused, those who revile your good behavior in Christ may be put to shame" (1 Pet. 3:16).

1. Why should you always maintain good conduct?

2. Do those who see you in gym class, at work and during play practice get a good impression of Christians?

Do as I Say, Not as I Do

Bruchko, the story of Bruce Olson, is the autobiography of a man
whom many would consider a "spiritual giant." It tells of a
nineteen-year-old boy who obeyed God's call to bring God's Word to
the Motilone Indians, a fierce jungle tribe of Colombia. He left the
U.S. with seventy dollars in his pocket. Once in Colombia, he had to
learn two languages before he even approached the Motilones.
When he did, they tried to kill him. He got tapeworms and suffered
other health problems from eating unsanitary food such as grub
worms. But he willingly gave up everything to follow Jesus.

Yet, in spite of all this, he was keenly aware of his failures. He
recognized the sin in his life. When discouraged, he thought of the
missionaries he had been critical of, he found the Bible boring, and
he doubted his calling.[2] Those who live very close to God, people
whom others consider saints, sense their sin and their guilt and their
failure more strongly than others.

Jesus was different. He felt no need to confess any sin. The New
Testament describes some of the temptations He faced but He
didn't yield to any of them. He had no sense of moral failure, no
guilt, but He was quick to recognize sin in others. In a debate with
the Pharisees, He said, " 'And he who sent me is with me; he has
not left me alone, for I *always* do what is pleasing to him. *You are of
your father the devil*' " (John 8:29, 44).

He once said to the religious rulers, " 'Woe to you, scribes and
Pharisees, hypocrites! for you are like whitewashed tombs, which
outwardly appear beautiful, but within they are full of dead men's
bones and all uncleanness. So you also outwardly appear righteous
to men, but within you are full of hypocrisy and iniquity" (Matt.
23:27-28).

He taught His disciples to pray, " 'And forgive us our debts, as
we also have forgiven our debtors' " (Matt. 6:12), but in His prayer
to His Father, He said, " 'I glorified thee on earth, having accomplished the work which thou gavest me to do'" (John 17:4).

Everyone hates a "do-as-I-say, not-as-I-do" teacher, but Jesus
was loved and respected. His disciples willingly gave their lives for
Him. And, you must admit, if Jesus is God, these statements imme-

diately make sense. All men were sinners, but He was perfect. He had no sense of moral failure because *He never failed.*

There is victory over sin for the Christian, but at the same time, the closer a person gets to God, the more sensitive he becomes to sin in his own life. According to James 4:17, "Whoever knows what is right to do and fails to do it, for him it is sin." This verse implies that *deliberate* disobedience is quite different, in God's eyes, from *unconscious* sin. As we learn more about God and get closer to Him, He shows us the critical attitude or the lack of patience of which we had been unaware. This should not upset us. The brighter the light, the more clearly the imperfections show up. This is the process of becoming more like Jesus. We simply confess the sin as we become aware of it, then stop doing it. The Holy Spirit will give us power to keep from deliberately rebelling against God.

"But the path of the righteous is like the light of dawn, which shines brighter and brighter until full day" (Prov. 4:18).
"But if we walk in the light, as he is in the light, we have fellowship with one another, and the blood of Jesus his son cleanses us from all sin" (1 John 1:7).

1. List the things that happen to us as we come closer to Jesus the Light of the World.
2. How can we become more holy and at the same time more conscious of sin?
3. What condition must be met in order for us to receive forgiveness?
4. Are you willing to stay very close to Jesus or do you want forgiveness *and* the right to run your own life?

A Goddess Doesn't Have to Apologize

"I'm just kidding." "I'm sorry, I didn't mean it that way." "I guess I didn't make myself clear." You've probably made statements like these. Everybody has—except Jesus. He never apologized for *anything* He said. He didn't need to because He always spoke the whole truth—clearly.

When Jesus said, " 'I and the Father are one' " (John 10:30), the Jewish listeners took up stones to throw at Him. After all, their law required stoning as the punishment for blasphemy. And if Jesus had

been merely human, His words would have been blasphemy. But notice that Jesus didn't quickly say, "Oh, I—I meant that God and I are one in, ah, purpose."

When the Jewish listeners explained, " 'We stone you for . . . blasphemy; because you, being a man, make yourself God,' " Jesus did not smooth over the situation. He replied, " 'If I am not doing the works of my Father, then do not believe me; but if I do them, even though you do not believe me, believe the works, that you may know and understand that the Father is in me and I am in the Father" (John 10:33, 37, 38). His listeners then tried to arrest Him, but Jesus escaped.

Because Jesus said, " 'My Father is working still, and I am working,' " "the Jews sought all the more to kill him, because he not only broke the sabbath but called God his Father, making himself equal with God" (John 5:17-18).

"The reason is that Jesus said, '*my* Father' not 'our Father,' making himself equal with God; on a par with God's activity. The Jews did not refer to God as 'my Father.' Or if they did, they would qualify the statement with 'in heaven.' However, Jesus did not do this. He made a claim that the Jews could not misinterpret when He called God 'my father.' "[5]

Jesus did *not* try to soften the impact of His words. His next statement was, " 'For as the Father raises the dead and gives them life, so also the Son gives life to whom he will. The Father judges no one, but has given all judgment to the Son, that all may honor the Son, even as they honor the Father' " (John 5:21-23). Any doubt as to whether or not Jesus claimed equality with God would be cleared up by this statement!

When Jesus said, " 'Truly, truly, I say to you, before Abraham was I am,' " He was using the personal name for God revealed in Exodus 3:14. And when the Jews prepared to stone Him, He didn't yell, "You didn't understand what I meant!" He ran and hid (John 8:58-59).

When the high priest at Jesus' trial asked, " 'Are you the Christ, the Son of the Blessed?' " Jesus not only referred to himself by using God's personal name, "I am," but added, " 'You will see the Son of man sitting at the right hand of Power, and coming with the clouds of heaven' " (Mark 14:61-62). When the high priest tore his clothes and cried, "Blasphemy!" Jesus said nothing to modify His declaration—and He was on trial for His life.

Jesus claimed to be equal with God and He stuck by His guns because it was true. However, we sometimes forget that His refusal to apologize, or to ever say, "I'm sorry," was an indirect claim to deity. At times, though, there are teenage and adult "gods" running around with an "I'm always right" complex. If your "a-goddess-doesn't-have-to-apologize" philosophy has been hurting other people, there may not be anybody around to stone you, but you'd better stop a minute to consider what God thinks of such an attitude.

"He leads the humble in what is right, and teaches the humble his way" (Ps. 25:9).

1. How long has it been since you've made a prayerful "attitude check"?
2. Are there attitudes God wants you to change and people to whom He wants you to apologize?
3. Can God teach you anything or do you know it all, already?

The Cross and the Crown

Those who argue that Jesus was not God are quick to point out that Jesus said, " 'The Father is greater than I' "; that He prayed to His Father, " 'Not my will, but thine, be done' "; that on the cross He cried, " 'My God, my God, why hast thou forsaken me?' " However, to deny that these words came from One who was equal with God is to miss the point of Jesus' coming to earth.

King Edward VIII of England fell in love with a woman who was not of royal blood and was unfit to be the Queen of England. He voluntarily gave up his wealth and his throne to marry the woman he loved. Once in exile, he was no less intelligent, no less of royal blood, and no less capable of ruling a country than before. But he had voluntarily limited himself.

In order to save us, Jesus did far more. In John 17, Jesus talks to God about " 'the glory which I had with thee before the world was made.' " Jesus had given up everything to be born into this world. "Though he was in the form of God, [He] did not count equality with God a thing to be grasped, but emptied himself, taking the form of a servant, being born in the likeness of men. And being found in human form he humbled himself and became obedient unto death, even death on a cross" (Phil. 2:6-8).

He who created everything became a creature. He who gave the law became subject to its demands. He who could have called armies of angels endured insults from the Pharisees and misunderstanding from His friends. And then, He, the Author of Life, allowed himself to be painfully executed as a criminal. Jesus sacrificed everything.

The writer of Hebrews, describing Jesus' life, writes, "But we see Jesus, who for a little while was made lower than the angels, crowned with glory and honor because of the suffering of death, so that by the grace of God he might taste death for every one" (Heb. 2:9). During His time on earth Jesus could truthfully say, "The Father is greater than I." Notice that, "for a little while," Jesus limited himself so much that even angels could do things He could not do. But God "raised him from the dead and made him sit at his right hand in the heavenly places" (Eph. 1:20). "Therefore God has highly exalted him and bestowed on him the name which is above every name, that at the name of Jesus every knee should bow, in heaven and on earth and under the earth, and that every tongue confess that Jesus Christ is Lord, to the glory of God the Father" (Phil. 2:9-11).

Now do you see that Jesus, the Word that was with God in the beginning, the Word that was God, had lost nothing of His deity, even though He laid aside His power and glory to come to earth? Jesus is now the hero of heaven because He conquered sin, death and the devil.

Just as Jesus gave up all His rights in order to do God's will, God is asking you to give up yours—the right to plan your own future, to be respected by everyone, and to quit whenever you want, must be exchanged for the life Jesus will give you. The cross came before the crown and it always will.

"But rejoice in so far as you share Christ's sufferings, that you may also rejoice and be glad when his glory is revealed" (1 Pet. 4:13).

"If we endure, we shall also reign with him; if we deny him, he also will deny us" (2 Tim. 2:12).

1. What is the difference between sharing Christ's sufferings and experiencing other suffering?
2. Do you fall apart when hard times come, or do you realize that the Jesus who suffered is in a perfect position to help you?

Made of the Right Stuff

Jesus was unquestionably divine, but we must never forget that He was fully human. He sat at Jacob's well because He was tired. He fell asleep in a boat during a raging storm. He wept when He saw the grief of others at the tomb of Lazarus. He felt disappointment when His disciples argued over who would be the greatest. He felt the sting of Judas' betrayal and the burden of praying alone while His best friends slept.

But Jesus was the *perfect* man and in that sense is "the first-born of all creation"—the first of those made of the stuff that could inherit heaven. He is also "the first-born from the dead"—the first to display a perfect body that would last forever. "Since therefore the children [people on earth] share in flesh and blood, he himself likewise partook of the same nature, that through death he might destroy him who has the power of death, that is, the devil, and deliver all those who through fear of death were subject to lifelong bondage" (Heb. 2:14-15).

"Therefore, if any one is in Christ, he is a new creation" (2 Cor. 5:17). The wonderful truth is that Jesus became man and died for us so that He could give to us His nature and promise us a resurrected body like His. Because of this, Jesus even has called us His brothers and sisters: "For those whom he foreknew he also predestined to be conformed to the image of his Son, in order that he might be the first-born among many brethren" (Rom. 8:29). Jesus gives us His own Spirit of life to sanctify us and make us holy. Therefore, "he who sanctifies and those who are sanctified have all one origin. That is why he is not ashamed to call them brethren" (Heb. 2:11).

The "image of the invisible God" who created all things became "the first-born of all creation" to impart this supernatural life to us. Now "his divine power has granted to us all things that pertain to life and godliness" (2 Pet. 1:13) and He will give us a new body like His own. "But our commonwealth is in heaven, and from it we await a Savior, the Lord Jesus Christ, who will change our lowly body to be like his glorious body, by the power which enables him even to subject all things to himself" (Phil. 3:20-21). We are joint heirs with Christ! How can we ever thank Jesus enough for giving himself totally to us so that we can share His glory? That is what Paul was referring to when he wrote, "Christ in you, the hope of glory" (Col. 1:27).

"He is the image of the invisible God, the first-born of all creation; for in him all things were created, in heaven and on earth, visible and invisible, whether thrones or dominions or principalities or authorities—all things were created through him and for him. He is before all things, and in him all things hold together. He is the head of the body, the church; he is the beginning, the first-born from the dead, that in everything he might be pre-eminent. For in him all the fulness of God was pleased to dwell, and through him to reconcile to himself all things, whether on earth or in heaven, making peace by the blood of his cross" (Col. 1:15-20).

1. What things in the above passage show that Jesus is God?
2. Because Jesus became "the first-born of all creation" and the "first-born from the dead," what things can He give to us?
3. Are you living like one of Christ's "new creations," who will some day have a heavenly body like His, or are you allowing yourself to be bogged down by boring classes and family problems?

Others Worshiped Jesus—Do You?

Peter walked thirty miles from Joppa to Cæsarea to tell Cornelius about Jesus. When Cornelius met him, he fell down at his feet and worshiped him. Peter was shocked and pulled him to his feet, exclaiming, " 'Stand up; I too am a man' " (Acts 10:25-26). Peter displayed the typical attitude of a Jewish person during the time of Jesus.

However, many people worshiped Jesus and He didn't tell them to stop. The wise men worshiped the baby Jesus but not Mary or Joseph. Jesus quoted from the Old Testament, " 'You shall worship the Lord your God and him only shall you serve' " to the devil, but accepted the worship of His disciples after He had stilled a storm. The man who had been born blind worshiped the Jesus who healed him, as did the demon-possessed man who lived among the tombs. The disciples worshiped the risen Jesus. Doubting Thomas exclaimed, " 'My Lord and my God.' "[7] And Jesus "rebuked Thomas for his unbelief, not for his worship."[8]

Jesus never told anyone not to worship Him. In fact, on the first Palm Sunday when the crowds were shouting, " 'Blessed is the King who comes in the name of the Lord!' " some crabby Pharisees who had forgotten their ear plugs asked Jesus to restore peace and quiet. Jesus replied, " 'I tell you, if these were silent, the very stones would cry out' " (Luke 19:38-40).

This not only proves that Jesus claimed to be God but that He demands our reverence, our honor, and our praise. Jesus deserves our worship, our love, and our adoration.

Worship and adoration come quite naturally to us—we're made with a desire to worship someone. If this need we have for worshiping becomes perverted, we find ourselves worshiping a rock star, a baseball player, or some girlfriend or boyfriend. When the person proves unworthy of that kind of adoration, we fall apart. Sometimes we nearly worship Christian leaders and when they disappoint us, we consider giving up Christianity. We can only be fulfilled as we love and adore and worship *Jesus*. He is the only One who will *never* let us down.

" ' "You shall worship the Lord your God and him only shall you serve" ' " (Matt. 4:10 [quoting Deuteronomy 6:13]).

"Now when Jesus was born in Bethlehem. . . , behold, wise men from the East came . . . to worship him. . . . And going into the house they saw the child with Mary his mother, and they fell down

and worshiped him" (Matt. 2:1, 2, 11).

"And when they got into the boat, the wind ceased. And those in the boat worshiped him, saying, 'Truly you are the Son of God' " (Matt. 14:32-33).

"Jesus . . . said, 'Do you believe in the Son of Man?' He answered, 'And who is he, sir, that I may believe in him?' Jesus said to him, 'You have seen him, and it is he who speaks to you.' He said, 'Lord, I believe'; and he worshiped him" (John 9:35-38).

"And when he saw Jesus from afar, he ran and worshiped him; and crying out with a loud voice, he said, 'What have you to do with me, Jesus, Son of the Most High God?' " (Mark 5:6-7).

"Now the eleven disciples went to Galilee, to the mountain to which Jesus had directed them. And when they saw him they worshiped him; but some doubted" (Matt. 28:16-17).

1. Why do these verses prove the deity of Jesus? (You may want to read them in context to get Jesus' reaction in each case.)
2. What person or thing do you actually worship? Does Jesus want to share your worship with someone else?
3. Take some time right now to adore Jesus, to tell Him how much you love Him, and to enjoy His presence.

Week Ten

FACT OR FICTION

The Not-So-Great Compromise

Let's face it. God's coming in human form to die for man's sins is beyond our imagination—and our logic! Many people are unwilling to admit that their reasoning cannot match God's. Instead of letting God be God and accepting His truth by faith, they make up a new theory, a compromise, that makes more "sense" to them. They create their own God, one whom they would rather worship.

Arius of Alexandria, Egypt, in the fourth century A.D., decided that Jesus was the first thing created by God and, therefore, a second god, inferior to God the Father. Others have attempted such compromise also. Some teach that Jesus was Michael the archangel, or some other created being.

People who insist that God must be governed by logic which can be substantiated with our sight insist that a person, including God, *must* be a solid physical mass. The Hebrew word for "one," *Echod*, used in the famous biblical prayer, " 'Hear, O Israel: The Lord our God is one Lord,' " is also used in Genesis where God declares that a married couple become "one flesh." It is also used to describe the cluster of grapes the spies brought back from Canaan. The Bible uses the word "one" to describe a "composite unity."[1] We have such a unity in Genesis 1:26: "Then God said, 'Let *us* make man in our image, after our likeness."

Just because it's hard for us to understand how God as the Father, Son and Holy Spirit can be a unity and yet be three persons is no reason to doubt what the Bible teaches. The age-old way of handling ignorance is making fun of something one doesn't understand. When people make fun of the Trinity and try to explain things logically, they are actually making up their own God. When they say, "Who was in heaven when Jesus died on the cross?" they refuse to acknowledge that the Bible teaches that Jesus and God are separate persons.

You should study and try to understand all that you can. But when you reach the limits of human logic, admit it—and believe God. If you refuse to accept spiritual truth which cannot be fully understood, you will end up compromising and believing unbiblical doctrine. Pray about the things you don't understand and ask God to give you light, but don't presume that your great intelligence will fill in all the gaps.

"He [Jesus] is before all things, and in him all things hold together" (Col. 1:17).

"In many and various ways God spoke of old to our fathers by the prophets; but in these last days he has spoken to us by a Son, whom he appointed the heir of all things, through whom also he created the world. He reflects the glory of God and bears the very stamp of his nature, upholding the universe by his word of power. When he had made purification for sins, he sat down at the right hand of the Majesty on high, having become as much superior to angels as the name he has obtained is more excellent than theirs. For to what angel did God ever say, 'Thou art my Son, today I have begotten thee'? . . . And again, when he brings the first-born into the world, he says, 'Let all God's angels worship him.' Of the angels he says, 'Who makes his angels winds, and his servants flames of fire.' But of the Son he says, 'Thy throne, O God, is for ever and ever' " (Heb. 1:1-8).

1. List all the facts the above verses reveal about Jesus.
2. Which statements show that Jesus isn't and never was an angel?
3. Which statements show that Jesus is indeed God?
4. Are you willing to pray about the things you don't understand and let God be God?

Mind-Boggling

I was teaching Mexican twelve-year-olds the English version of a Russian story about a boy and a goat who sought shelter in a huge haystack during a blizzard. But most of my students had seen neither snow nor a haystack. And the language was not their own! I began to appreciate the fact that spiritual truths, which are beyond the grasp of man, must be expressed in human language and thought in the Bible.

It is clear that Jesus was and is completely God: "In him [Christ] the whole fulness of deity dwells bodily" (Col. 2:9).

"There is no possibility of translating this verse in any other way. It is not just 'the fulness' of deity, it is 'The whole fulness.' There is no kind of deity which He did not have. Likewise, it is not merely a temporary but a permanent possession of deity—not just in the eternal Lord but in the historical Jesus ('bodily') that the fulness of deity is to be found."[2]

There are those who would say that Jesus is referred to as the Son of God because He is less than God, but this is not true to the facts. God has to express divine truth in human terms. The closest human equivalent to the loving relationship between God and Jesus, who was sent by His Father to do His Father's will, is that of father and son.

This, of course, is not to be taken literally—it would be absurd to search for God's wife! We also know that God is not literally a rock, a shepherd, or a shield, even though these terms are used in the Bible to describe Him.

Saying that Jesus was the Son of God does not mean that He was a created being, a "secondary god." In several Bible passages we find that Jesus is recognized as Creator of the world. For example, Hebrews 1:2 states, "He has spoken to us by a Son, . . . through whom also he created the world." C. S. Lewis explains that the difference between the Creator and a created one is so great that it makes the difference between an archangel and a worm quite insignificant.[3]

If you recite the Apostles' Creed in your church, each Sunday you say, "I believe in Jesus Christ, His only Son our Lord." You declare that Jesus is God, for that is what "Lord" means in the New Testament. You may not understand it completely, but it is important to accept *all* of God's truth, even if it's mind-boggling at times. Avoid the temptation to leave out, or reinterpret a few scripture passages in order to manufacture a neatly packaged "truth" which is easy to swallow. You need not be uncomfortable with your inability to mentally grasp all of God's plan. But we can say with the Psalmist, "How great are thy works, O Lord! Thy thoughts are very deep!" (Ps. 92:5).

"O the depth of the riches and wisdom and knowledge of God! How unsearchable are his judgments and how inscrutable his ways! 'For who has known the mind of the Lord, or who has been his counselor?' 'Or who has given a gift to him that he might be repaid?' For from him and through him and to him are all things. To him be glory forever" (Rom. 11:33-36).

1. Do you trust God enough to thank Him for the things you don't understand?
2. Jesus told us that the Holy Spirit will guide us "into all truth." Do you ask the Holy Spirit to reveal God's truth to you, rather than depending on your brains?
3. Spend some time praising God for sending Jesus to this earth.

Mission Accomplished

A lot of religious groups claim that although Jesus was a good fellow, someone else had to come and bring a deeper revelation of God. That revelation has come in many forms, depending on the religion: as a series of visions received by Mohammed (Islam), as golden plates written in "reformed Egyptian" "translated" by Joseph Smith and then misplaced (Mormonism), as the writings of Baha'u 'lla (Bahai), or as the teaching that some new Messiah must come as the Lord of the Second Advent (Unification). They all contradict what Jesus said about himself and what the Bible teaches.

We read in 2 Peter 1:2-3: "May grace and peace be multiplied to you in the knowledge of God and of Jesus our Lord. His divine power has granted to us *all* things that pertain to life and godliness." Jesus has given us everything we need, and the teaching of any other person is completely unnecessary.

Neither John the Baptist nor anyone else hindered Jesus from fulfilling His mission. In fact, John the Baptist referred to Jesus as one " 'the thong of whose sandal I am not worthy to untie' " (John 1:27), and said of His Master, " 'He must increase, but I must decrease' " (John 3:30). Jesus told His Father, " 'I glorified thee on earth, having *accomplished* the work which thou gavest me to do' " (John 17:44). And cried from the cross, "It is *finished*" (John 19:30). The ultimate revelation was complete.

It is dangerous to add to the words of God; the Bible tells us: " 'You shall not add to the word which I command you, nor take from it; that you may keep the commandments of the Lord your God" (Deut. 4:2). Notice that this verse does not say that God had stopped giving His commandments in the written form. It only cautions against changing them in any way. In the last chapter of Revelation, the final book of the New Testament, we find a warning about altering the Word of God: "I warn every one who hears the words of the prophecy of this book: if any one adds to them, God will add to him the plagues described in this book, and if anyone takes away from the words of the book of this prophecy, God will take away his share in the tree of life" (Rev. 22:18-19).

In Romans 5 we read that the sin of Adam caused the whole human race to suffer death and other effects of sin. But because of the death and resurrection of Jesus Christ all can be forgiven and have eternal life: "For if many died through one man's trespass, much more have the grace of God and the free gift in the grace of that one man Jesus Christ abounded for man. Then as one man's trespass led to condemnation for all men, so one man's act of righteousness leads acquittal and life for all men" (Rom. 5:15, 18). There is no need for anyone else to come.

Paul, in 1 Corinthians 15, his famous chapter on the resurrection of Jesus, explains that even though "we have borne the image of the man of dust, we shall also bear the image of the man of heaven." We will have bodies like the resurrected body of Jesus. Here he contrasts Jesus with Adam, explaining that " 'the first man Adam became a living being' " and the last Adam (Christ) became a "life-giving spirit," able to give eternal life to others. As we know, Adam was made from dust but Jesus is the man from heaven who will return some day to give those who follow Him imperishable and immortal bodies. Jesus came to save us and to give us eternal life. He is God in the flesh, the complete revelation of God—and He accomplished His mission.

"For no other foundation can any one lay than that which is laid, which is Jesus Christ" (1 Cor. 3:11).

"But you are fellow citizens with the saints and members of the household of God, built upon the foundation of the apostles and prophets, Christ Jesus himself being the cornerstone" (Eph. 2:19-20).

1. Why is it wrong for someone to claim a revelation from God which contradicts Jesus or tries to give Him second place?
2. Do you ever let someone's advice have more importance than the words of Jesus?

Twenty-four-Hour Service

Could you imagine having a priest kill a cow or a pigeon every time you sinned? You would relive the episode of your talking back to your mother as you looked into the innocent brown eyes of Daisy, your favorite cow, and watched the priest shove a knife into her. Aren't you glad that this is no longer needed?

The Bible teaches that after Jesus died on the cross, the priests which descended from Aaron, of the tribe of Levi, were no longer necessary. When Jesus died, the curtain of the temple was torn in two from top to bottom, indicating that God did the tearing, and that it is no longer necessary for the priest to enter the most holy part of the temple with a special sacrifice each year. Hebrews 7-10 explains that Jesus is now our permanent high priest, " 'a priest for ever, after the order of Melchizedek.' "

Hebrews 7:22-25 says, "This makes Jesus the surety of a better covenant [agreement]. The former priests were many in number, because they were prevented by death from continuing in office; but he holds his priesthood permanently, because he continues forever. Consequently he is able for all time to save those who draw near to God through him, since he always lives to make intercession [pray] for them."

Although Jesus replaced the priests descended from Aaron, by making them unnecessary, He was from the tribe of Judah; He was literally fulfilling the prophecy: " 'You are a priest for ever after the order of Melchizedek' " (Ps. 110:4). When Abraham returned home after rescuing Lot from a pagan army, he was met by Melchizedek, the priest-king of Jerusalem, then called Salem. The writer of Hebrews explains that since Abraham, the ancestor of Aaron, paid tithes (10% of his wealth) to Melchizedek, his priesthood was much greater than that of Aaron. Since Jesus has been given the office of " 'a priest forever, after the order of Melchizedek,' " and He will never die, no one else can become heir to this position.

No one today can be a priest after the order of Aaron or after the order of Melchizedek. There is no place for secret services, rituals, mysteries, and the idea that a person needs a special priest in order to find God. (This is not to be confused with the *position* of priest, pastor or minister which simply indicates that a person is a leader in a certain church.) Because the job of priest was to take the sacrifice and to be a "middleman" between God and the people, there is a sense in which every true Christian is a priest. Since Jesus died, we can go directly and ask forgiveness for our sins without a sacrifice, and therefore perform the function of priest for ourselves. Martin Luther called this "the priesthood of all believers." We can also pray for others and show them how to discover fulfillment and eternal life. The apostle Peter declares, "But you are a chosen race, a royal priesthood, a holy nation, God's own people, that you may declare the wonderful deeds of him who called you out of darkness into his marvelous light" (1 Pet. 2:9).

But we are priests only in the sense that we need no special person or group of people to arrange for our forgiveness or our instruction. We still need our High Priest, the "one mediator between God and men, the man Christ Jesus" (1 Tim. 2:5).

"Since then we have a great high priest who has passed through the heavens, Jesus, the Son of God, let us hold fast our confession. For we have not a high priest who is unable to sympathize with our

weaknesses, but one who in every respect has been tempted as we are, yet without sinning. Let us then with confidence draw near to the throne of grace, that we may receive mercy and find grace to help in time of need" (Heb. 4:14-16).

1. List all the qualifications possessed by Jesus our High Priest.
2. Do you go to Jesus asking for grace and mercy or do you just do the best you can?

The Worst Thing You Can Think Of

Christianity has been called a "butchershop religion." Many people object because a blood sacrifice for sin seems barbaric and primitive. It doesn't appeal to the modern mind. There are also those who say that Jesus' blood was just as effective in His veins as it was dripping to the ground below the cross.

One of the easiest ways to discover if the doctrines of a religious group are truly Christian is to find out what the group believes about the blood of Jesus. (Much terminology is designed to be deceptive, so to know the true position of the group, you must find out what their terms actually mean.) Only the blood of the perfect Son of God, who died on a cross, can provide forgiveness. Such a doctrine no religion would *invent.*

People don't like to think that their sin is so bad that the death of a person, the shedding of blood, is required to cleanse them. They much prefer to view their imperfections as "human errors" which can be paid for by following a set of rules, living a good life, or performing certain rituals. The person who first said, "God helps those who help themselves," has a bigger following than the Bible. After all, no one likes to feel so rotten and hopeless that only the blood of another can eradicate his or her sin.

But this is just what the Bible teaches. God gave garments of skin to Adam and Eve. An animal had been killed and its blood poured out as a sacrifice for their disobedience. When Abel offered a lamb to God, his sacrifice was accepted, but the fruit and vegetables given by Cain were rejected because no blood was involved. Abraham sacrificed animals to God as did other great men of the Bible. The Law of Moses instituted a sacrificial system to atone for the sins of the people.

Hebrews 9:22 tells us: "Indeed, under the law almost everything is purified with blood, and without the shedding of blood there is no forgiveness of sins." Leviticus 17:11 tells us that this is because the life is in the blood. We deserve to die for our sin and only the death of another can remove our sin. Jesus himself said it when He instituted the Lord's Supper: " 'This is my blood of the covenant, which is poured out for many for the forgiveness of sins' " (Matt. 26:28).

We may not fully understand how, but the blood of Jesus cleanses and purifies and protects. "The blood of Jesus his Son *cleanses* us from all sin" (1 John 1:7); "how much more shall the blood of Christ . . . *purify* your conscience from dead works to serve the living God" (Heb. 9:14); " 'they have *conquered* him [the devil] by the blood of the Lamb and by the word of their testimony' " (Rev. 12:11). When Satan tries to harass you, don't argue with him. Remind him of the blood of Jesus.

Certainly the cross was messy and horrible and painful. It showed us how bad our sin really is and that only blood can atone for it. If you're ever tempted to go right ahead and do something, even though you know it's wrong, remember that it's just like sticking the sword into the side of Jesus, or driving the nail deeper into His wrist. Sin should be the worst thing you can think of.

"Let not sin therefore reign in your mortal bodies, to make you obey their passions. Do not yield your members to sin as instruments of wickedness, but yield yourselves to God as men who have been brought from death to life, and your members to God as instruments of righteousness" (Rom. 6:12-13).

1. If your mind and every part of your body are not given to God, what automatically takes over?
2. Have you declared war on the sin in your life?
3. Commit yourself to obeying God and ask Him for the power to defeat sin.

More Than a Forgiveness Factory

Jesus was not a martyr. He did not die because the religious leaders and the Romans finally got the better of Him. He *gave* His life as the perfect sacrifice for our sins, as had been planned by God and prophesied throughout the Old Testament. "But he was wounded for our transgressions, he was bruised for our iniquities; . . . All we like sheep have gone astray; we have turned every one to his own way, and the Lord has laid on him the iniquity of us all" (Isa. 53:5-6).

Jesus was our substitute on that cross. We all deserve that penalty but He took our place. "Christ died for our sins in accordance with the scriptures" (1 Cor. 15:3). But Jesus did not die so that we could just accept His forgiveness and go on sinning, living any way we choose. Some believe this. Sadly, they give the critics of Christianity reason to say that those who believe in salvation by works do more to help the world than Christians do.

God's granting salvation apart from holy living is like a man offering to give his heart for transplanting into a patient who continues in alcoholism, smoking, temper tantrums and wrong eating habits—the very things that destroyed the first heart—and made life miserable for everyone else.

Paul was shocked that anyone would even think that Jesus' death for our sins means we can keep sinning and sinning just to take full advantage of the forgiveness of Jesus. He says, "Are we to continue in sin that grace may abound? *By no means!*" (Rom. 6:1). The basic selfishness of the heart-transplant patient must be adequately dealt with, or his new heart will soon be ruined.

When Jesus died on the cross, that selfish part of us that wants its own way was crucified with Him. "We know that our old self was crucified with him so that the sinful body might be destroyed, and we might no longer be enslaved to sin" (Rom. 6:6). We received the forgiveness of Jesus by faith—faith not only in the power of Jesus to forgive sin, but faith in His power to keep us from committing the same sins over and over.

In the same way, we identify with the death of Jesus by believing that our old sinful self was crucified with Him. By faith we let that become real in our lives as we obey God at every point, no matter what the price. Calvary is more than a forgiveness factory. It is our participation in Jesus' death, the crucifixion of our evil desires and our inclination to be little gods who control everything. But Jesus also rose in power and glory. And as we yield our sinful selves to crucifixion, the Holy Spirit's resurrection power for victorious living is ours as well.

"What then? Are we to sin because we are not under law but under grace? By no means! Do you not know that if you yield yourselves to any one as obedient slaves, you are slaves of the one whom you obey, either of sin, which leads to death, or of obedience, which leads to righteousness? But thanks be to God, that you who were once slaves of sin have become obedient from the heart to the standard of teaching to which you were committed" (Rom. 6:15-17).

1. What would you say to the person who says, "It doesn't matter if I sin, I can always be forgiven"?
2. What is the difference between obedience from the heart and outward conformity to God's commandments? Where does power to obey come from?
3. Do you really want to obey God or are you still holding out on a few issues?

"Abracadabra, Amen"

Our fantasies die quickly. Children outgrow letters to Santa Claus. And grown-ups realize that neither the president nor the queen can do anything about the weather, pneumonia, or making someone fall in love with Susie. It's ridiculous to ask anyone but God to fundamentally change people or to untangle complicated situations. No person would be so crazy as to tell others that he or she was able to do anything that people asked.

But Jesus said, " 'Whatever you ask in my name, *I* will do it, that the Father may be glorified in the Son; if you ask anything in my name, *I* will do it' " (John 14:13-14). No one but God could dare make a promise like this. Jesus was teaching people to pray to Him. And New Testament people did pray to Jesus. In his dying breath, Stephen said, " 'Lord Jesus, receive my spirit' " (Acts 7:59). John ends the book of Revelation with the prayer, "Amen. Come, Lord Jesus!"

The New Testament doesn't teach that praying to Jesus is only praying in His name. When Jesus himself said, "If you ask anything *I* will do it," He personally promised that *He* will answer our prayers. Therefore we need to discover what it means to pray in Jesus' name.

Obviously, praying in the name of Jesus does not mean that we'll get anything we ask for if we use the magic formula, "in Jesus' name, Amen," instead of abracadabra! We must remember that a person's name stands for all that the person is. When a person is asked to sign his or her name, it's a total commitment—to stick by the rules or to come up with the money. And you cannot use a person's name without permission.

You don't use the name of a person to ask for something that's not consistent with the person behind the name. Most of you would not think of saying, "Dad, please give me a million dollars," because most of your fathers do not have that kind of money. Neither do you ask, "Sally, will you help me kill the neighbor's dog?" because you know Sally loves animals. Praying, "Jesus, make all the trees turn purple so I can get my name in the newspaper," would be unthinkable. Before you use a person's name to ask for something, you must *know* that person. Then your petition will be consistent with the character of that person.

When you pray in the name of Jesus, remember that He has all power. Also, remember that you have to get to know Jesus well enough so that you know what to pray for. Read His Word and spend time with Him. You'll find out that He won't help you get straight A's without studying. But you'll discover that He wants to help you in many things—if you'll only *obey* Him.

"I write this to you who believe in the name of the Son of God, that you may know that you have eternal life. And this is the confidence which we have in him, that if we ask anything according to his will he hears us. And if we know that he hears us in whatever we ask, we know that we have obtained the requests made of him" (1 John 5:13-15).

1. Whom does this passage tell us to pray to?
2. What is the prerequisite for getting real answers to our prayers?
3. How can you learn to pray according to the will of Jesus?

Week Eleven

SOME HISTORY WAS WRITTEN BEFORE IT HAPPENED

Your God-in-the-Box Doesn't Work Right

The life of Jesus fulfilled Old Testament prophecies to the letter. Someone has even advanced a theory that Jesus, who knew about these prophecies, engineered His life in such a way as to fulfill them. There are, however, some problems with this theory—it's rather hard to determine the circumstances of one's birth and to decide to rise from the dead!

Even the first prophecy in the Bible tells us something about the birth of Jesus. After the devil deceived Eve in the Garden of Eden, God said to the serpent (the devil), " 'I will put enmity between you and the woman, and between your seed and her seed; he shall bruise your head, and you shall bruise his heel' " (Gen. 3:15).

"In all of Scripture, only one Man was 'born of the seed of a woman'—all others are born of the seed of a man."[1] Since He had no human father and His death and resurrection conquered Satan in the same way that a fatal blow to the head defeats a snake, Jesus literally fulfilled this prophecy.

Micah, in the Old Testament, predicted that the Messiah would be born in Bethlehem: "But you, O Bethlehem Ephrathah, who are little to be among the clans of Judah, from you shall come forth one who is to be ruler in Israel, whose origin is from of old, from ancient days" (Mic. 5:2). How fitting for the Messiah, who was promised the throne of David, to be born in Bethlehem, the "City of David." Think of the number of cities and villages in the world! God eliminated all of them and chose Bethlehem, with less than 1,000 inhabitants, to be the birthplace of His Son.

Jesus was the only baby born who existed before His conception—"whose origin is from of old"—He was the Divine Messiah who would eventually come a second time to rule, not only Israel, but the world.

The religious rulers of Israel knew about this prophecy. When the wise men came to Jerusalem, the scholars gladly showed off their knowledge. They knew that the Messiah was to be born in Bethlehem and they quoted the right scripture to prove it. But they didn't go to worship Him and they didn't believe in Jesus when He grew up. They had their doctrine, their interpretation. They expected a certain kind of Messiah who would come in a certain way. They had picked out all the verses about His being a king and ignored the ones which told of His suffering and death. Because Jesus didn't fit into the box they had constructed for Him, they said, "Forget it."

Many times we make the same mistake. We lose our "faith" if our pet poodle dies despite our prayers for his recovery, or if the person we respected as a Christian falls into sin. But God isn't wrong. Our ideas about prayer are wrong.

As we carefully study the lives of Bible characters, we realize that God does not promise ease and comfort to those who follow Him. Each time our system fails, we must come to God humbly and ask Him to teach us from His Word. We must be careful not to miss Jesus because He doesn't fit our expectations.

Your "God-in-the-Box" just might not work right!

"When they heard these words, some of the people said, 'This is really the prophet.' Others said, 'This is the Christ.' But some said, 'Is the Christ to come from Galilee? Has not the scripture said that the Christ is descended from David, and comes from Bethlehem, the village where David was?' So there was a division among the people over him" (John 7:40-43).

1. These people knew that Jesus grew up in Nazareth and assumed He was born there. Why do you suppose they didn't find out where Jesus was *really* born?
2. Why didn't they bother to look up the prophecy which says the Messiah would spend time in Galilee?
3. Do you check out your preconceived notions with the facts of Scripture? Are you willing to let God change your ideas?

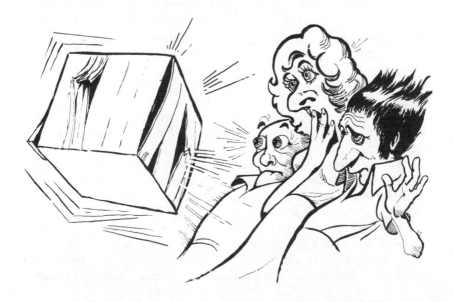

Kingdom Kids in the Valley

The sign, "The King of the Jews," nailed above Jesus on the cross, seemed a cruel joke to some and an impossibility to others. Those who rejected Jesus as the Messiah failed to realize that, at that point, many prophecies had been fulfilled, *and* that Jesus would come again as King to fulfill the rest of them. The prophecies of the Old Testament are not labelled "First Coming" and "Second Coming." Most of those who read the Old Testament made the mistake of thinking that all the prophecies about the Messiah would be fulfilled at one time.

Mountains and valleys might provide a useful illustration at this point. When you're driving along a road, it's possible to see what looks like a huge mountain up ahead. But when you get closer, you discover that your mountain is really two mountains with a valley in between. The prophecies about Jesus are like that. There are two "mountains" of prophecies with a "valley" between them. Some were fulfilled the first time He came and He is coming again as King to fulfill the rest of them.

God promised David, "And your house and your kingdom shall be made sure for ever before me; your throne shall be established for ever" (2 Sam. 7:16). After the Babylonians took the Jews captive in 587 B.C., they were never again ruled by a descendant of David. But even before the hope of an enduring earthly kingdom ruled by the dynasty of David was gone, Isaiah, the prophet, had made it clear that this prophecy would be fulfilled through one Person. He wrote, "For to us a child is born, to us a Son is given; and the government will be upon his shoulder, and his name will be called 'Wonderful Counselor, Mighty God, Everlasting Father, Prince of Peace.' Of the increase of his government and of peace there will be no end, upon the throne of David, and over his kingdom, to establish it, and to uphold it with justice and with righteousness from this time forth and for evermore" (Isa. 9:6-7). Only a divine Messiah could fulfill this prophecy.

In Luke 3 the ancestry of Mary is traced back to Nathan, a son of David. Humanly speaking, Jesus was therefore a "son of David." Matthew 1 shows us that Joseph, Jesus' legal father, was also a descendant of David and heir to his throne.

But this prophecy was not to be fulfilled the first time that Jesus came. There was a valley between the two mountains. The first time, Jesus came to suffer and die as a fulfillment of some of the prophecies. But He himself predicted His second coming. He said,

" 'When the Son of man comes in his glory, and all the angels with him, then he will sit on his glorious throne' " (Matt. 25:31). He will come again as king.

If you really know Jesus, His coming again is that mountain beyond the valley that seems so tough and boring. When your team loses twelve games straight, when your parents cancel the family vacation because of lack of money, and when your church youth group falls apart, you can remember that Jesus is coming again as King. And a "Kingdom Kid" couldn't have a brighter future.

"Looking to Jesus the pioneer and perfecter of our faith, who for the joy that was set before him endured the cross, despising the shame, and is seated at the right hand of the throne of God" (Heb. 12:2).

1. What should we think about when we become discouraged?
2. Talk to Jesus about any frustrations you are now facing.

Before You Throw Your Own Pity Party . . .

Do you feel that no one understands you and that every kid in school has "got it together," except you? Does it seem that you can't be popular without a "Drugs, Sex, and Rock-n-Roll" t-shirt?

Well, just remember that Jesus went through even tougher things, so He knows how you feel. This fact about His life was prophesied. Isaiah 53:3 says, "He was despised and rejected by men; a man of sorrows, and acquainted with grief; and as one from whom men hide their faces he was despised, and we esteemed him not." John 1:11 explains the New Testament fulfillment of that prophecy: "He came to his own home, and his own people received him not."

People spread lies about Jesus in order to ruin His reputation. One of His closest friends betrayed Him. A thousand years before Christ, David wrote, "Even my bosom friend in whom I trusted, who ate of my bread, has lifted his heel against me" (Ps. 41:9). Judas ate the last supper with Jesus before betraying Him, thus fulfilling the prophecy.

But Jesus did not become depressed. He did not give up or feel like a failure. He knew God's will for His life and realized that nothing else mattered. And He died, not only to forgive our sins, but to break the power of sin in the world—to give love to the unloved person, to free people from the habits that have chained them, and to heal the hurts we have suffered at the hands of others.

That is one of the most important reasons that Jesus came. "The Spirit of the Lord God is upon me, because the Lord has anointed me to bring good tidings to the afflicted; he has sent me to bind up the brokenhearted, to proclaim liberty to the captives, and the opening of the prison to those who are bound" (Isa. 61:1). When Jesus stood up to read in the synagogue at Nazareth, He chose that scripture and explained it, saying, " 'Today this scripture has been fulfilled in your hearing' " (Luke 4:21).

Instead of a robot world in which sin and its dreadful consequences are impossible, God chose to give people free will. He then provided a way of remolding the clay of their lives—no matter how marred—into beautiful examples of His grace. There is a sense in which Calvary absorbed all the heartache in this world. Jesus wants to wipe away our tears and comfort us. But we let self-pity and fear and hatred prevent God's healing from flowing into our lives. The people who really trust God for their lives display a "walking on the water attitude" in spite of handicaps, shattered families, and tragedy.

Maybe you're even an "If-God-can-save-that-guy,-He-can-save-anybody" advertisement; but if you'll give that life to Jesus, He'll make something wonderful out of it. And don't get discouraged when the molding process hurts. Jesus is there to help you. He knows exactly how it feels.

"So I went down to the potter's house, and there he was working at his wheel. And the vessel he was making of clay was spoiled in the potter's hand, and he reworked it into another vessel, as it seemed good to the potter to do. Then the word of the Lord came to me: 'O house of Israel, can I not do with you as this potter has done? says the Lord' " (Jer. 18:3-6).

1. Who makes the beautiful vase, the clay or the potter?
2. Who is responsible for making you into a beautiful person, you or God?
3. You are living clay, so you can refuse to be made into that beautiful vase. What things do you do to hinder God's working?

Palm-Sunday Christians Are Good-Friday Traitors

Jesus had entered Jerusalem many times before. But this time it would be different. He wasn't going to walk in with His disciples. He told them where to find the donkey and the exact words to say to his owner so they could borrow him. After they had brought the donkey to Jesus, they made a saddle out of their coats and Jesus rode into Jerusalem. As Jesus entered the city, people spread garments and palm branches on the way and Jesus rode over them. They cheered. " 'Hosanna! Blessed is he who comes in the name of the Lord!' " (Mark 11:9).

Jesus was so poor that He had to borrow the donkey. However, riding on a donkey "is quite in keeping in biblical thought with a royal personage coming peaceably."[2] This event fulfilled Zechariah 9:9: "Rejoice greatly, O daughter of Zion! Shout aloud, O daughter of Jerusalem! Lo, your king comes to you; triumphant and victorious is he, humble and riding on an ass, on a colt the foal of an ass." This was Jesus' deliberate declaration of himself as the Messiah. The people responded with joy.

Jesus was also affirming the kind of Messiah He was. He did not come on a horse with a battle cry of "Death to the Romans." He came in peace and humility to conquer *sin*, not the Roman Empire.

Jesus knew His mission and His reason for living. The people did not. Jesus intended to carry out the will of His Father, no matter what the cost. The cheering of the crowds, the political oppression and the easiest way out did not sway Him.

However, the people wanted to follow a Messiah who would require nothing difficult of them. On Palm Sunday, when the sun was shining and Jesus was popular, they shouted their hosannas. But, later that week, many of these same people were yelling, "Crucify him! Crucify him!" Those who didn't openly deny Him went into hiding. Not one person was willing to defend Him.

If you have not made a full surrender to Jesus, you will always be a Palm-Sunday Christian. But such Easy Street Christianity won't make it. God doesn't promise you that you can marry the person *you* want to marry, get the job *you* want to have, or even live where tin-roof sundaes are always available. He doesn't guarantee a life without problems.

You can't follow Jesus unless you give up your right to have your own way. When the Good Fridays come along, you've got to be more than a Palm-Sunday Christian.

"But recall the former days when, after you were enlightened, you endured a hard struggle with sufferings, sometimes being publicly exposed to abuse and affliction, and sometimes being partners with those so treated. For you had compassion on the prisoners, and you joyfully accepted the plundering of your property, since you knew that you yourselves had a better possession and an abiding one. Therefore do not throw away your confidence, which has a great reward. For you have need of endurance, so that you may do the will of God and receive what is promised" (Heb. 10:32-36).

1. Compare the cost of your being a Christian with what it cost the Hebrew Christians.
2. Which is easier, going through a crisis or enduring day after day? Why?
3. Why do we need endurance?
4. Are you a Palm-Sunday Christian or are you willing to go with Jesus all the way?

A Pet Lamb Makes History

Events of the Old Testament, as well as words, form prophecies. The significant Feast of the Passover is such a prophecy. The Israelites had been slaves in Egypt for four hundred years. They were overworked and underpaid. God sent Moses to lead them out of Egypt, but even after hail, fire, grasshoppers and flies, Pharaoh would not let them go. In order to force Pharaoh to release the Israelites, God decided that the firstborn child of each family in Egypt would have to die. No deaths would occur in Israelite families if each household would follow God's directions by killing and eating a perfect lamb. But this wasn't just eating Woolly Willie the pet lamb for supper. This was history in the making. The blood of the lamb was to be placed on the doorposts to save the firstborn from death. Each lamb was to be roasted without breaking any of its bones and to be completely eaten with bitter herbs. All leftovers were to be burned. No Israelites died that fateful night, and the Jews have faithfully kept the Passover ever since.

Jesus is compared to the perfect Passover lamb, without spot or blemish, whose blood is the only means for our salvation. In Isaiah 53 we read, "Like a lamb that is led to slaughter, and like a sheep that before its shearers is dumb, so he opened not his mouth. . . . Yet it was the will of the Lord to bruise him; . . . when he makes himself an offering for sin" (Isa. 53:7, 10).

John the Baptist said of Jesus, " 'Behold, the Lamb of God, who takes away the sin of the world!' " (John 1:29).

Jesus' blood, like the blood of the Passover lamb, offers the only hope of salvation, and in heaven people thank Jesus for dying for them "The twenty-four elders fell down before the Lamb, . . . and they sang a new song, saying, 'Worthy art thou. . . , for thou wast slain [killed] and by thy blood didst ransom men for God from every tribe and tongue and people and nation' " (Rev. 5:8-9).

The Passover lamb was killed between 3:00 p.m. and sundown. This custom has been followed, according to the Jewish historian Josephus, in all succeeding Passover celebrations. According to the Gospel of Matthew, Jesus died about the ninth hour (3:00 p.m.) or shortly afterward. John's gospel tells us it was the day of preparation (of the Passover). Thus, we see that Jesus, the Lamb of God, died exactly at the time that the Passover lamb was to be killed.

Just as the Israelites were not to break a bone of their Passover lamb, no bone in Jesus' body was broken. The Jews did not want bodies hanging on the crosses during Passover, so they asked Pilate to have the soldiers break the legs of the victims, which would cause them to die immediately. "So the soldiers came and broke the legs of the first, and of the other who had been crucified with him; but when they came to Jesus and saw that he was already dead, they did not break his legs" (John 19:32-33). This not only completes the prophetic event of Passover, it fulfills Psalm 34:20 as well: "He keeps all his bones; not one of them is broken."

Passover also teaches us something more about Jesus. The roasted lamb of Passover was to be eaten with bitter herbs, symbolizing repentance. All was to be eaten and the leftovers burned. The fire represents Jesus' enduring of God's anger against sin so that we could be forgiven. But His sacrifice does not affect our lives until our repentance is real and we want all of Jesus.

It's easy to want Christ's forgiveness, but not His commandments; His love, but not His demands; and His peace, but not His burden. The Passover lamb was not for taste-testing. Neither can Jesus be partially accepted. It's all or nothing.

"And he said to all, 'If any man would come after me, let him deny himself and take up his cross daily and follow me' " (Luke 9:23).

1. Is your love for football, popularity or nice clothes keeping you from taking all of Jesus and following Him completely?

2. Are the things that *Jesus* wants more important to you than the
   things that *you* want?

Jesus' Death and Your Life

Before crucifixion was even practiced, the death of Jesus was described in Psalm 22: "I am poured out like water, and all my bones
are out of joint; my heart is like wax, it is melted within my breast;
my strength is dried up like a potsherd [broken piece of pottery],
and my tongue cleaves to my jaws; thou dost lay me in the dust of
death. Yea, dogs are round about me; a company of evildoers encir-
cle me; they have pierced my hands and feet—I can count all my
bones—they stare and gloat over me; they divide my garments
among them, and for my raiment they cast lots."

It probably took less than an hour of hanging on the cross for
Jesus' bones to pull out of joint.

The Bible uses the word "dogs" to describe detestable people.
Those who stood by the cross that day, the ones who had yelled,
"Crucify him! crucify him!" and those who came to mock must
have seemed like wild dogs, drooling for the kill. The *Encyclopaedia
Britannica* explains that the arms of those crucified were nailed
firmly to the cross through the wrists and that the feet were fastened
with a nail through each foot.[3] As the hands and feet of Jesus were
pierced, the pain made Him aware of each bone in His body. The
soldiers took Jesus' clothes but decided not to tear His tunic, so they
cast lots to see who would get it. When Jesus was crucified, the
prophecy of the Psalmist was fulfilled exactly.

Only crucifixion, a form of execution used by Persians and Selu-
cids as well as Romans, could have caused Jesus' hands and feet to
have been pierced. Those who say that Jesus was impaled on a
stake go against prophecy and against history. The dictionary says
that to impale is "to pierce or pierce through with a pole or with
something pointed, to torture or kill by fixing on a sharp stake."
Obviously, to kill someone this way the stake would have to punc-
ture the vital organs, not the hands and feet. The Bible also states
that not one of Jesus' bones was broken, and it would be difficult to
impale someone without breaking any bones.

A real Jesus died a real death on a real cross as prophesied in the
Old Testament. Judas Iscariot was not crucified in His place and
His death was not an illusion. "The death of Jesus was not just an
ideal or a symbol but a fact of space and time. . . . Jesus died in the
same sense that, if you had been there that day, you could have

rubbed your finger on the cross and gotten a splinter in it."[4]

Imagine the resounding blow of the hammer and the intense pain inflicted each time the nail was hit. The Carpenter, who was also the Son of God, allowed four nails to seal His death. He who had power over not only nails but over storms, leprosy and death permitted wicked men to nail Him to a cross because He loved *you* and wanted to save you.

"While we were yet helpless, at the right time Christ died for the ungodly. Why, one will hardly die for a righteous man—though perhaps for a good man one will dare even to die. But God shows his love for us in that while we were yet sinners Christ died for us" (Rom. 5:6-8).

1. Have you ever *thoughtfully* read the story of the crucifixion (Matt. 26, 27) and thanked Jesus for each thing He suffered for you?
2. Why would anything Jesus asks you to give up for Him seem like a small sacrifice in comparison to Calvary?
3. Are you willing to let your whole life be a "thank you" to Jesus for dying for you?

One in 100,000,000,000,000,000!

The Old Testament prophets accurately predicted the details of Jesus' life hundreds of years before He was born.

The first two verses of Isaiah 9 explain that the land near the Sea of Galilee, occupied by the tribes of Zebulun and Naphtali (which had recently been destroyed by an Assyrian king), would in the future be blessed by the presence of the Messiah, "the Light of the World." "But there will be no gloom for her that was in anguish. In the former time he brought into contempt [being looked down upon] the land of Zebulun and the land of Naphtali, but in the latter time he will make glorious the way of the sea, the land beyond the Jordan, Galilee of the nations. The people who walked in darkness have seen a great light; those who dwelt in a land of deep darkness, on them has light shined."

The New Testament tells about Jesus working in this area. "And leaving Nazareth he went and dwelt in Capernaum by the sea, in the territory of Zebulun and Naphtali, that what was spoken by the prophet might be fulfilled" (Matt. 4:13-14).

Malachi 3:1 prophesied the coming of John the Baptist to prepare the way for Jesus: " 'Behold, I send my messenger to prepare the way before me, and the Lord whom you seek will suddenly come to his temple.' " In Matthew 11:10, Jesus said of John the Baptist, " 'This is he of whom it is written, "Behold, I send my messenger before thy face, who shall prepare thy way before thee." ' "

The prophet Malachi also declared that the Lord would come to His temple. "Malachi 3:1 and four other Old Testament verses require the Messiah to come while the temple of Jerusalem is still standing. This is of great significance when we realize that the temple was destroyed in A.D. 70 and has not since been rebuilt."[5]

Isaiah 53:9 gives us details about the death of Jesus: "And they made his grave with the wicked and with a rich man in his death, although he had done no violence, and there was no deceit in his mouth." Those who crucified Jesus with thieves tried to condemn him to a criminal's grave, but "a rich man from Arimathea, named Joseph, . . . went to Pilate and asked for the body of Jesus. . . . Joseph took the body, . . . and laid it in his own new tomb" (Matt. 27:57-60).

According to the principles of mathematical probability, the chances of one man being born who would fulfill just *eight* of the Old Testament prophecies concerning Jesus are one in 100,000,000,000,000,000![6] We can only bow in worship and adoration before the God who so carefully planned for Jesus to come to be our Way of Salvation. God has not changed. His wonderful plan is being worked out in your life as well. You can mess things up with your disobedience and resistance, but He still has a way of straightening out all the tangled threads and weaving them into another matchless design if you just let Him do it.

"Though I formerly blasphemed and persecuted and insulted him; but I received mercy because I had acted ignorantly in unbelief, and the grace of our Lord overflowed for me with the faith and love that are in Christ Jesus. The saying is sure and worthy of full acceptance, that Christ Jesus came into the world to save sinners. And I am the foremost of sinners; but I received mercy for this reason, that in me, as the foremost, Jesus Christ might display his perfect patience or an example to those who were to believe in him for eternal life" (1 Tim. 1:13-16).

1. How did God work out His plan in the life of the Apostle Paul, even though Paul had once been an enemy of Jesus?
2. How can Paul's life with Jesus be an example for you?
3. Are you willing to let an all-knowing God work out His design for your life, or do you have your life planned?

Week Twelve

WHY ALL THE FUSS OVER AN EMPTY TOMB?

A Whole Week Off from School

The school calendar may read "Spring Recess," and the dates may not coincide perfectly with Easter, but everybody still knows that it's really *Easter* Vacation. According to the *Encyclopaedia Britannica,* "Easter's origins go back to the beginnings of Christianity and it is probably the oldest Christian observance of the kind after Sunday, which was regarded as the weekly celebration of the resurrection."[1] The earliest writings about Easter concern discussions on whether it should be celebrated on Sunday or on whichever weekday Passover fell. A second-century bishop named Polycrates of Ephesus argued for his position by citing the tradition in Ephesus and the practice of the Apostle John. This proves that the celebration of Easter goes back to the earliest days of the Church.

The origin of our English word Easter is a matter of controversy. Some have connected it with an Anglo-Saxon goddess called Eostre who personified the east, morning and spring. Even if this could be proven, it would not mean much since English was not the original language of Christianity. Pascha is the word for Passover in Greek, the language in which the New Testament was originally written. The words for Easter in Spanish (Pascua) and French (Pâques) come from this origin.

Just as with Christmas; certain pagan customs have become integrated into the Easter tradition. Ancient people such as the Persians and the Egyptians used the egg as a symbol of fertility and new birth. The egg later became a Christian symbol of the resurrection.

You may prefer an Easter without eggs and you may even want to call it Resurrection Day, but it is ridiculous to discount it because some ancient Christians decided to endue a possibly pagan name and a pagan symbol with Christian meaning. Why do some people pretend to be so concerned about the pagan goddess who may have given her name to a Christian holiday? They want to hide the fact that Jesus rose from the dead. But the biblical accounts, which are read and studied annually, make it quite difficult for people to believe their new doctrine that Jesus was raised only "in the spirit." Peter's statement in his first sermon, " 'This Jesus God raised up, and of that we are all *witnesses*' " (Acts 2:32), makes no sense if Jesus was merely raised "in the spirit." What would there be to "witness"?

The study of the events of Easter should not only keep you from wrong doctrine but should give meaning to your life. How about using some time during that week of "spring" vacation to ponder one of the greatest lessons of history? On the first Easter, God turned history's greatest defeat into its greatest victory. Satan thought he had triumphed. Jesus' enemies thought they were finally rid of Him. But God was still in control. Jesus conquered Satan by His death and resurrection. Because of the resurrection, you can always deal with the devil as a defeated enemy.

"He raised him (Jesus) from the dead and made him sit at his right hand in the heavenly places, far above all rule and authority and power and dominion, and above every name that is named, not only in this age but also in that which is to come; and he has put all things under his feet and has made him the head over all things for the church, which is his body, the fulness of him who fills all in all" (Eph. 1:20-23).

1. Explain, in your own words, the position Jesus is in because of His resurrection.
2. Since you're part of the body of Christ and all things have been put under the feet of Jesus, what is your position?
3. For what problem do you need to claim the victory of Jesus right now?

Three Days and Three Nights Is Not a Six-Man Rock Group

On Good Friday millions pause to consider Jesus' suffering and death on the cross. It is good to have a special time to remember and to appreciate what Jesus did for us.

As a child, not understanding the victory of the cross, I thought it should be called "Bad Friday." As a teenager without much knowledge of Hebrew culture, I wondered how Jesus could have been crucified on Friday, raised on Sunday and still have spent three days in the tomb.

Jesus prophesied, " 'For as Jonah was three days and three nights in the belly of the whale, so will the Son of man be three days and three nights in the heart of the earth' " (Matt. 12:40). When asking Pilate for a guard for the tomb, the Pharisees said, " 'Sir, we remember how that imposter said, while he was still alive, "After three days I will rise again" ' " (Matt. 27:63).

There are two ways of approaching the problem. Halley takes the first approach when he points out that "in Hebrew usage parts of days at the beginning and the end of a period were counted as days" and that in Matthew 27 "the third day" is used as an equivalent to "after three days." He suggests that three days and three nights is a long way of saying three days.[2]

Another explanation goes like this: If we assume that Jesus was crucified on Friday we also suppose that the Sabbath of the Passover fell on Saturday, the weekly Sabbath. This may not necessarily be the case. Sabbath means "rest day"; the word is used to describe other Jewish holidays. In Leviticus 16, where the rules are established for the Day of Atonement which fell on different days of the week, as did Passover, this observance is described as " 'a sabbath of solemn rest to you.' "

Some Bible scholars believe that Jesus ate the Last Supper on Tuesday night of our week (Wednesday for the Hebrew calendar because their days started at sundown) and that this meal may not have been the Passover supper. John 19:14 tells us that Jesus was crucified on the "day of Preparation of the Passover; . . . about the sixth hour" (noon). He died about 3:00 p.m. (the ninth hour), just as the Passover lambs were being killed, and was buried before sundown on the Day of Preparation, before the Passover was eaten (John 19:42; Matt. 27:59-60). This would be Wednesday evening of our week, which would mean He spent Thursday, Friday, and Saturday in the tomb. Jesus could have risen from the dead any time after the sun went down on Saturday night because the "first day of the week" began at sundown on our Saturday. Matthew 28 only tells us that Sunday morning the angel rolled the stone away and said, " 'He is not here; for he has risen.' "[3]

Although it is good to know that there are logical explanations for the apparent contradiction of Good Friday, it is important to have a time to remember the Savior who made history with the words " 'not as I will, but as thou wilt.' "

"And going a little farther he fell on his face and prayed, 'My father, if it be possible, let this cup pass from me; nevertheless, not as I will, but as thou wilt' " (Matt. 26:39).

1. How would history have been different if Jesus had not prayed this prayer?
2. Much is lost, in terms of God's kingdom, every time you refuse to pray this prayer. What is God asking you to do right now that is against *your* will?

It Takes a Lot of Faith to Disbelieve

The resurrection of Jesus has got to be history's most unusual event. People just don't rise from the dead every day or every century! That people should disbelieve is to be expected. However, the kinds of explanations they invent to avoid the resurrection show that it's a lot easier to believe that Jesus rose from the dead.

In the eighteenth century, a guy by the name of Venturini thought up the "swoon theory." According to Venturini, Jesus, after a hard day at the hill, fainted on the cross. He looked dead, so was placed in the tomb. After three days in the dark, cold tomb with no food, water or medical care, He rallied His strength. He promptly performed the superhuman feat of rolling the stone away, then proceeded to travel about, making surprise appearances to convince people that He had risen from the dead.

However, in all the ancient writings which condemn Christianity, there is not one *hint* that anyone ever considered such a swoon theory.

In addition, there are recorded facts that just don't fit the theory. John writes, "But one of the soldiers pierced his side with a spear, and at once there came out blood and water. He who saw it has borne witness—his testimony is true, and he knows that he tells the truth—that you also may believe" (John 19:34-35). This is *medical* proof of death, recorded by an eyewitness. Besides, those Roman soldiers were pretty good at crucifixions. They'd had practice.

Also, no man, after enduring crucifixion, could have made the appearance described in John 20:19: "On the evening of that day, the first day of the week, the doors being shut where the disciples were, for fear of the Jews, Jesus came and stood among them and said to them, 'Peace be with you.' " A man who had survived trial, mockery, flogging, and crucifixion, and had been three days without food and water would have sent his followers scurrying for a doctor rather than evoking the response of the women who "came up and took hold of his feet and worshiped him" (Matt. 28:9).

Finally, if the swoon theory were true, Jesus would be a big liar, a heartless man who sent others to a martyr's death just because He wanted people to believe He was the Son of God. Very few enemies of Christianity ascribe to Jesus that kind of cruelty.

But there is something the swoon theory can teach us: the life of a cynic is a hard one. After years of unbelief, no reason or moral sense is left. It always starts slowly but it gets progressively worse. Watch for signs of hardness and unbelief in your life and deal with them before they get out of control.

"As I urged you when I was going to Macedonia, remain at Ephesus that you may charge certain persons not to teach any different doctrine, nor to occupy themselves with myths and endless genealogies which promote speculations rather than the divine training that is in faith; whereas the aim of our charge is love that issues from a pure heart and a good conscience and sincere faith" (1 Tim. 1:3-5).

1. What does Paul warn Timothy against?
2. Why is any topic which promotes speculation and endless discussion not worth your time?
3. What is the aim of proper Christian teaching?
4. Is there an area of unbelief in your life which is dragging you down?

Tomb Watching Can Be Exciting

Can you imagine a job more boring than spending a night guarding a corpse in a cemetery? Well, it didn't turn out that way for some men of the first century. The temple leaders who engineered His crucifixion remembered that Jesus had predicted His own resurrection. They asked Pilate for guards to insure that the disciples would not steal the body and proclaim to the world that Jesus had risen from the dead. "Pilate said to them, 'You have a guard of soldiers; go, make it as secure as you can' " (Matt. 27:65).

A most amazing thing happened. By Sunday morning the tomb was empty. Matthew tells us why "graveyard shift" guard duty was so exciting: "And behold, there was a great earthquake; for an angel of the Lord descended from heaven and came and rolled back the stone, and sat upon it. His appearance was like lightning, and his raiment white as snow. And for fear of him the guards trembled and became like dead men" (Matt. 28:2-4). The tomb was empty.

The empty tomb was acknowledged by the *enemies* of the early Christians, as well as by their friends. Even Josephus, a *Jewish* historian, wrote, "He appeared to them alive again the third day."[4] And you'll notice that the enemies of the early Church never attempted to disprove the resurrection. They simply got mad.

The case of the empty tomb is strengthened by the fact that no

pilgrimages or visits to that tomb are ever recorded. Although there are some good reasons for believing that the Church of the Holy Sepulchre in Jerusalem is built over the tomb of Jesus, no one can be completely positive. The tomb of Jesus had not been important to the early Christians.

The first invented explanation for the empty tomb proves that the enemies of Jesus were hard up for excuses. "And when they had assembled with the elders and taken counsel, they gave a sum of money to the soldiers and said, 'Tell people, "His disciples came by night and stole him away while we were asleep." And if this comes to the governor's ear, we will satisfy him and keep you out of trouble' " (Matt. 28:12-14). However, the death penalty was required of a Roman soldier sleeping while on guard duty, so it is doubtful that those soldiers would have slept. If the men came from the priests' temple guard as some scholars believe, it's still rather strange that they could verify what happened while they were sleeping!

The empty tomb was bound to change history, regardless of those who disbelieved. It was to offer a message of hope to the world. Jesus said it in a nutshell: " 'Because I live, you will live also' " (John 14:19).

" 'For this is the will of my Father, that every one who sees the

Son and believes in him should have eternal life; and I will raise him up at the last day' " (John 6:40).

"He who believes in the Son has eternal life; he who does not obey the Son shall not see life, but the wrath of God rests upon him" (John 3:36).

1. How does the resurrection of Jesus affect us?
2. Why can Jesus give us eternal life?
3. Have you accepted His offer?

Linen and Spice

The Jews did not bury a corpse in his best suit as we do today. They wrapped a body in long strips of cloth, soaked with spices. Evidently it was the custom to make a special kind of cap for the head. John describes Lazarus, whom Jesus raised from the dead, as he came out of the tomb, "his hands and feet bound with bandages, and his face wrapped with a cloth" (John 11:44). Now, they didn't just stick in a few cloves as they wrapped the body. We read that "Nicodemus also, who had at first come to him by night, came bringing a mixture of myrrh and aloes, about a hundred pounds' weight. They took the body of Jesus, and bound it in linen cloths with the spices, as is the burial custom of the Jews" (John 19:39-40). Even if they had washed the body (as Luke records was done with the body of Dorcas—Acts 9:37), it is likely that blood and fluid from the wounds would have matted this heavy cocoon to the dead body.

It didn't take a Sherlock Holmes to see that the tomb wasn't completely empty that first Easter morning. The evidence left in the tomb is what first made John believe that Jesus had risen from the dead. John described what happened after he and Peter had a race to the tomb. Using the third person to refer to himself, he said: "But the other disciple outran Peter and reached the tomb first; and stopping to look in, he saw the linen cloths lying there, but he did not go in. Then Simon Peter came, following him, and went into the tomb; he saw the linen cloths lying, and the napkin, which had been on his head, not lying with the linen cloths but rolled up in a place by itself. Then the other disciple, who reached the tomb first, also went in, and he saw and believed" (John 20:4-8).

Once the body was gone, the linen cocoon collapsed. However, the headcovering or napkin, still in its place, must have maintained its helmet shape due to the crisscross pattern of the bandages. John wrote of Mary Magdalene, "She saw two angels in white, sitting where the body of Jesus had lain, one at the head and one at the feet" (John 20:12). In both Matthew and Mark the women are invited to see the place where Jesus had lain—to view the evidence of the grave clothes. "A glance at these graveclothes proved the reality, and indicated the nature of the resurrection. They had been neither touched nor folded nor manipulated by any human being. They were like a discarded chrysalis from which the butterfly had emerged."[5]

God is concerned about details and ordinary things. He used linen and spice as evidence of His Son's resurrection. He'll use the little ordinary things in your life to prove to others that the risen Jesus is living in *you*. He'll use a smile for a lonely old lady, an attitude of obedience when your mother is unreasonable, or a cheerful manner when you get stuck cleaning up someone else's mess. Don't wait for that big opportunity to show off your Christianity. It'll never come. God uses linen-and-spice evidence to display His power if that linen and spice is dedicated to Him.

"And they were bringing children to him, that he might touch them; and the disciples rebuked them. But when Jesus saw it he was indignant, and said to them, 'Let the children come to me, do not hinder them; for to such belongs the kingdom of God. Truly, I say to you, whoever does not receive the kingdom of God like a child shall not enter it.' And he took them in his arms and blessed them" (Mark 10:13-16).

1. Why were the disciples upset when people brought their children to Jesus?
2. Are you too busy doing important things to notice the thoughtful things you can do to bless others?
3. What impact do you suppose the blessing of Jesus had on those children?
4. Think about this scripture passage and then pray about it. If you are not serving God in the little details of your life, you are not serving Him.

"Ladies First"

Women played an important part in the resurrection drama. When reading the accounts of the resurrection in the Gospels, it's easy to get the idea that the tomb was a bit like Grand Central Station. Mourning women coming and going, frightened guards, angels, an unnamed young man, Peter and John, and who knows who else made their appearances. Wouldn't *you* run to see the tomb of a good friend who had reportedly risen from the dead? Curiosity is part of human nature.

Jesus appeared first to Mary Magdalene before He showed himself to any of His male disciples. John tells us that as Mary sat by the door of the tomb weeping, two angels asked her why she was crying. When Jesus asked her the same question, she turned to Him and answered that someone had taken Jesus' body—she thought He was a caretaker. Then He called her by name. She recognized the voice of Jesus and went to tell the other disciples that she had seen Him.

Someone has observed that John's account has to be true because no first-century male would have invented it! Mark also records it. The authors of the Gospels carefully explain that the women came to anoint the body of Jesus and that it was the women who first learned of the resurrection. They even give the names of these women with no hint that they were anything but reliable, sound-minded and honest. Only the men of *later* centuries have tried to discredit these women.

There are those who say that the weeping, distraught women went to the *wrong* tomb, which of course was empty. They then proceeded to use their talent for gossip so effectively that soon the whole world had heard of the "resurrection."

But consider some of the facts. First of all, the women knew where the tomb was because Mark says, "Mary Magdalene and Mary the mother of Joses *saw* where he was laid" (Mark 15:47).

Secondly, the wrong-tomb theorists claim Peter and John *also* went to the wrong tomb, and that Joseph of Arimathea, owner of the tomb, never bothered to straighten things out.

The "never underestimate the power of a woman" adage was not needed by the early Christians. After all, God had entrusted two of His most important messages to women. It was a woman who first received word that Jesus was to be born and it was women who first heard the glorious news of the resurrection. There were times when "ladies first" was part of God's plan.

"For in Christ Jesus you are all sons of God, through faith. For as many of you as were baptized into Christ have put on Christ. There is neither Jew nor Greek, there is neither slave nor free, there is neither male nor female; for you are all one in Christ Jesus" (Gal. 3:26-28).

1. How does the attitude toward women shown in the Bible run

contrary to the general view of that time?

2. Many problems arise in Christian living when we decide we are inferior or superior to any person or group. What attitude *should* we have?

3. Are you comparing your spirituality favorably or unfavorably with any person or group? What does God want you to do about this?

When Truth Proved Stranger Than Fiction

There was no need to prove to the enemies of Jesus that the tomb was empty. They knew it all too well. But, they didn't know what had happened to the body. Some said that the Jewish leaders or grave robbers stole the body. The only reason the temple leaders would want the body would be to display it, so the apostles would stop teaching this resurrection nonsense. They could have stopped Christianity instantly by producing the body of the man whom Christians claimed had risen from the dead.

What about grave robbers? Well, people don't break past armed guards, roll away a stone that three women knew they couldn't handle, and steal a body just for the fun of it. The only possible motive would have been the hope of receiving payment from the authorities. But the authorities obviously had no body to show off.

So the disciples got blamed. In Jerusalem, where the facts were known and people could check up on details, the story of the disciples stealing the body was probably not believed. However, it seemed pretty logical to those living in *other* cities. (United Press news releases had not been invented yet!)

Consider Paul (then Saul), the Christian-hunter. What would have made him so adamant against the preachers of the resurrection? He wasn't cruel, mean and awful for himself. He wrote, "If any other man thinks he has reason for confidence in the flesh, I have more: . . . a Hebrew born of Hebrews; . . . as to *zeal* a persecutor of the church, as to the righteousness under the law blameless" (Phil. 3:4-6). Paul believed that the disciples were liars, that they were deceiving people. If the disciples really had stolen the body and were running around preaching the resurrection, he had good reason for persecuting Christians. An honest man such as Paul hated to see innocent people being taken for a ride. The life of Saul proves that the Jewish authorities did not have the body and that the only explanation they could come up with was that the disciples stole it. When the star persecutor decided that the strange story of the resurrection was true and that the tale about the disciples stealing the body was false, he was put on the most-wanted list by the other persecutors.

Jesus has power to change a person completely and point him or her in the opposite direction. This can be seen clearly in Paul. Someone must have been praying for him to get converted. As you pray for your friend, or your father, or your atheist teacher, remember that God's power to change people has no limits.

"Now as he journeyed he approached Damascus, and suddenly a light from heaven flashed about him. And he fell to the ground and heard a voice saying to him, 'Saul, Saul, why do you persecute me?' And he said, 'Who are you, Lord?' And he said, 'I am Jesus, whom you are persecuting; but rise and enter the city, and you will be told what you are to do.' [Three days later he] was baptized. . . . For several days he was with the disciples at Damascus. And in the synagogues immediately he proclaimed Jesus, saying, 'He is the Son of God' " (Acts 9:3-6, 18-20).

1. What made Paul change his mind about Jesus and the resurrection?
2. Do you believe that God is able to change you and the people you are praying for?
3. Who should be your "faith project" for this month?

Week Thirteen

THE WORLD'S GREATEST HOAX

Do You Recognize Jesus?

We usually have little problem with what we *expect* to see. But, it often takes us a few moments to recognize even a person we know well, if we see him or her in a totally unexpected place, or if our minds are occupied with something else.

It is true that neither Mary Magdalene nor the disciples on the road to Emmaus recognized Jesus immediately. But is this reason to doubt that Jesus rose from the dead? One theory states that another man was asked to go about saying that he was the risen Jesus, just in case His plot to survive the crucifixion failed. Others say that the disciples wanted Jesus alive so badly that they imagined another man was Jesus.

These theories don't even tackle the problems of the empty tomb and what happened to the body. Also, if Jesus tried to deceive people, He would have been a fake, and that just doesn't square with His passion for justice and His sacrificial life. Consider also, that although people may be startled by seeing a familiar face in an unexpected circumstance, they do take an *extra* good look once they recognize who it is.

Mary Magdalene, whose eyes were blinded by tears, could easily not have recognized Jesus at first. And Luke says about the Emmaus incident, "Jesus himself drew near and went with them. But their eyes were *kept* from recognizing him" (Luke 24:15, 16). It seems that Jesus had an important Bible lesson to teach, and He didn't want His listeners distracted by the excitement of seeing Him alive.

It should be noted that there were other resurrection appearances in which people had no trouble recognizing Jesus. For instance, when Jesus appeared to the disciples, while they were hiding behind closed doors, He showed them His hands and feet and they immediately recognized Him.

But are there times when you also fail to recognize Jesus? Do you miss Him because you're too busy even to listen to the still, small voice that is saying, "Why are you doing all the things you're doing? Stop everything until you get your priorities straight and put *me* first." Or are you too wrapped up in your youth group activities to show kindness to a sick neighbor or that unpopular girl in your English class? Instead, you rush on, not seeing the hurt look in Jesus' eyes. Or do you ignore an opportunity to give to the poor because you "need" a new jogging suit and you don't hear Jesus saying, " ' "It is more blessed to give than to receive" ' "?[1] Jesus is there. You just don't recognize Him.

"Then he will say to those on his left hand, 'Depart from me, you cursed, into the eternal fire prepared for the devil and his angels; for I was hungry and you gave me no food, I was thirsty and you gave me no drink, I was a stranger and you did not welcome me, naked and you did not clothe me, sick and in prison and you did not visit me. Then they also will answer, 'Lord, when did we see thee hungry or thirsty or a stranger or naked or sick or in prison, and did not minister to thee?' Then he will answer them, 'Truly, I say to you, as you did it not to one of the least of these, you did it not to me' " (Matt. 25:41-45).

1. What excuses do you have for not recognizing what Jesus would have you do?
2. What does Jesus have to say about you and your clique ignoring the new kid in your youth group or the girl who just moved to your town from New York?
3. Are poor people in another part of the world your responsibility? How can you help them?

Why Die for a Lie?

If Jesus did not rise from the dead, the apostles were lying—and they knew it. They didn't just say, "We've been *taught* that our Savior is risen." They said, " 'But God raised him on the third day and made him manifest; not to all the people but to *us* who were chosen by God as *witnesses*, who ate and drank with him after he rose from the dead' " (Acts 19:40-41). They claimed to have seen Him, to have talked with Him, and even to have eaten with Him after He had risen from the dead.

Even though rising from the dead is a most unusual occurrence, it is illogical to accuse the disciples of lying. The Jewish chief priests tried it. They instructed the soldiers, " 'Tell people, "His disciples came by night and stole him away while we were asleep" ' " (Matt. 28:13). But the people didn't believe that the disciples were lying. The disciples were trustworthy men who held truth in high regard. They taught others to be honest and upright. Their standards were higher than those of other men.

Besides, if the disciples really made up the whole story, they were the most cruel men that had ever lived. They were asking others to give up possessions, to be ostracized by their families, and to face fierce persecution in order to follow the risen Jesus. As someone has observed, "The score in the Colosseum was lions six, Christians nothing." If the apostles were intentionally deceiving people, they were heartless.

No one accused the disciples of being crazy. Their lives were too well ordered and ethical for that. And it's psychologically impossible to believe that sane men would die for a lie they *originated*. People have died for lies that they thought were true, but that is different from dying for *known* falsehood. Eleven of the twelve apostles were martyred. If this was all a practical joke, at least one of them would have confessed rather than be stoned or crucified.

The apostles not only died in triumph, but they also lived victoriously in all kinds of adverse circumstances. They knew that Jesus rose to conquer sin, death and the devil. They knew that the Source of the power and victory of Jesus had become theirs as well.

"That the God of our Lord Jesus Christ, the Father of glory, may give you a spirit of wisdom and of revelation in the knowledge of him, having the eyes of your hearts enlightened, that you may know what is the hope to which he has called you, what are the riches of his glorious inheritance in the saints, and what is the immeasureable greatness of his power in us who believe, according to the working of his great might which he accomplished in Christ when he raised him from the dead and made him sit at his right hand in the heavenly places" (Eph. 1:17-20).

"But God . . . made us alive together with Christ (by grace you have been saved) and raised us up with him, and made us sit with him in the heavenly places" (Eph. 2:4-6).

1. What miracle is accomplished by the power of the Holy Spirit who dwells in the hearts of those who truly believe in Jesus?
2. Why do we need "the eyes of [our] hearts enlightened"? What do we need to *see*?
3. Notice that "God raised us up with him" so we can live in the victory of the resurrection of Jesus. In what situation do you need the faith to see God's great power work? Ask Jesus for this now.

No Unemployment Insurance for Pilate

Pilate was a wishy-washy governor who could have used a spine transplant. He tried to play both ends against the middle so he wouldn't find himself unemployed. The governorship of Palestine was about the worst job Rome had to offer, but, if he could just stick it out, there would be opportunity for advancement and prestige. So he washed his hands and said Jesus was innocent, as he allowed his soldiers to prepare for Him a criminal's death. Pilate's immediate aim was to prevent a riot and to keep influential people in Palestine from sending letters of complaint to Caesar.

Some people have accused Pilate or his Roman soldiers of stealing the body of Jesus. It certainly would have come in handy had Pilate possessed it—can you imagine his horror upon hearing that all Jerusalem was saying that Jesus was risen and that the tomb was empty? The Jews' strong hatred of Rome could make people forget completely that they had cried, "Crucify Him! Crucify Him!" and lay all the blame on Pilate and his Roman soldiers. A full-scale riot or a mailbox full of complaints about his rule could end his career. If Pilate had hidden the body, he certainly would have produced it quickly to set the score straight and keep himself safe. But he did not.

Pilate may have been the first Roman ruler to wonder what to do about Christianity, but he certainly wasn't the last. The Roman Empire just wasn't ready for the apostles. But have you ever stopped to think how a band of twelve uneducated men from a remote, provincial part of the Roman Empire could lead a movement which outlasted the empire itself? And they did it without armies. They also did it in the face of violent persecution from Jews and Romans. Only an experience as dramatic as seeing the risen Christ, and the realization that His victory over death offered eternal life to all, could have changed the whole Roman Empire and the world.

Because Jesus rose and conquered death, He offers eternal life to all who believe. His resurrection power is available to all who are fully surrendered to Him. These facts cease to amaze us. We've heard them too often without making them real in our lives. They've become just words. Jesus hasn't changed and the message hasn't changed. It's just that few, very few, really believe it.

"Then Peter, filled with the Holy Spirit, said to them, 'Rulers of the people and elders, if we are being examined today concerning a good deed done to a cripple, by what means this man has been healed, be it known to you all, and to all the people of Israel, that by the name of Jesus Christ of Nazareth, whom you crucified, whom God raised from the dead, by him this man is standing before you well. This is the stone which was rejected by you builders, but which has become the head of the corner. And there is salvation in

no one else, for there is no other name under heaven given among men by which we must be saved.' Now when they saw the boldness of Peter and John, and perceived that they were uneducated, common men, they wondered; and they recognized that they had been with Jesus" (Acts 4:8-13).

1. What things did Peter have to say about Jesus?
2. What did Peter's audience notice about Him?
3. Would a dead Jesus still in the tomb have given this same boldness to Peter?
4. Do you have such boldness to witness for Jesus? If not, who can give it to you?

Pink Elephants and a Picnic Breakfast

The Bible records that Jesus' disciples saw Him alive many times after His resurrection. The people who don't want to believe it have a story that goes like this: "Sure, they saw Him. People have also seen pink elephants and have had visions of Egyptian pharaohs."

The disciples, however, were not having hallucinations. In a hallucination, a person sees something that is not there. It usually happens at the end of a long period of wishing that a certain thing will occur. Both the crucifixion and the resurrection caught everyone off guard, so this could not be the case. Neither the burly fishermen nor doubting Thomas seem like good candidates for hallucinations. Their responses showed that they were surprised: "As they were saying this, Jesus himself stood among them. But they were *startled* and *frightened*" (Luke 24:36-37).

Hallucinations are highly individual and a whole group of people don't experience the same hallucination. Yet, Jesus appeared to *groups* of people. Paul says in 1 Corinthians 15:5-7, "He appeared to Cephas, then to the twelve. Then he appeared to more than five hundred brethren at one time, most of whom are still alive. . . . Then he appeared to James, then to all the apostles."

To have a hallucination, a well person must be in a thoughtful mood and in appropriate surroundings. But the post-resurrection appearances of Jesus occurred in a variety of settings: in the garden near the tomb, on a road as two disciples were walking, in the upper room, and at a picnic breakfast on the shores of the Sea of Galilee.

The breakfast by the Sea of Galilee was the worst possible environment for a hallucination. After tugging away at a net so full of fish that the seven of them were unable to pull it in, Peter jumped into the water to swim ashore. (The water in the Sea of Galilee is *cold*—I went swimming in it once.) All this activity would have jolted him into reality; and besides, the whole thing happened before an audience. The men all ate breakfast with Jesus (ever *eaten* with a hallucination?), and then Jesus had a long talk with Peter about his future. The Jesus Peter encountered that day was real.

But how real is Jesus to you? Is He just someone you imagine at times in a daydream, which could just as well include pink elephants and orange grass? Or do you talk over every detail of your life with Him, let Him help you with your homework, invite Him to go on dates with you and let Him tell you what to do with your life?

"Jesus said to him [Peter], 'Feed my sheep. Truly, truly, I say to you, when you were young, you girded yourself and walked where you would; but when you are old, you will stretch out your hands, and another will gird you and carry you where you do not wish to go.' (This he said to show by what death he was to glorify God.) And after this he said to him, 'Follow me.' When Peter saw him [John] he said to Jesus, 'Lord, what about this man?' Jesus said to him, 'If it is my will that he remain until I come, what is that to you? Follow me!' " (John 21:17-19, 21-22).

1. The real Jesus made some demands on Peter's life. What were they?
2. How is the Jesus of your imagination different from the real Jesus?
3. The real Jesus expects you to follow Him. In what areas is He asking you to make new surrenders to Him? Talk this over with Jesus.
4. Will you let Jesus tell you what to do with your life?

Three Thousand Murderers Admit Guilt

"Scaredy-cat Fisherman Turns into Dynamite Preacher." This would have made a good headline in the *Jerusalem Times* the day after Pentecost. The transformation of Simon Peter is amazing to say the least. The night before Jesus was crucified, Peter was such a chicken that he told a maid that he didn't even know Jesus. Fifty days later he stood up and boldly preached a sermon before all of Jerusalem. Imprisonment and an appearance before the "supreme court" didn't shake his courage. Two things had happened to Peter since he had denied Jesus: he had seen the risen Jesus and he had been filled with the Holy Spirit.

Not only the change in Peter, but the content of his message and the results of his sermon prove the resurrection of Jesus. He said; " 'This Jesus, delivered up according to the definite plan and fore-knowledge of God, you crucified and killed by the hands of lawless men. But God raised him up, having loosed the pangs of death, because it was not possible for him to be held by it. This Jesus God raised up, and of that we all are witnesses. Being therefore exalted at the right hand of God, and having received from the Father the promise of the Holy Spirit, he has poured out this which you see and hear' " (Acts 2:23-24, 32-33).

Can you imagine being in an audience and having the speaker accuse you of murder? Not only that, but the speaker is claiming that this murdered man has risen from death and is now seated at the right hand of God the Father Almighty. If anyone who cared to could walk over to the tomb and find the body, and if the resurrection of Jesus were not common knowledge, Peter would have been lynched. A crowd won't listen to a speaker who is accusing them of such a hideous crime unless he speaks the truth and unless their consciences are beginning to bother them.

Peter was not lynched by his audience. The crowd didn't jeer or hoot or pelt him with rotten eggs. Instead, they responded, " 'Brethren, what shall we do?' " (Acts 2:37).

At the very scene of the crime, where eyewitnesses could be questioned and the facts could be checked, people readily acknowledged their guilt of crying, "Crucify him! Crucify him!" They were guilty of murdering the Author of Life. About three thousand people accepted Jesus as Savior that day because the resurrection was irrefutable. They knew then that Jesus was the Son of God.

But Jesus' death and resurrection demands a response from you as well. You killed him, too, you know. It was for your sins that He died. He has every right to demand a life for a life. He gave His life for you. Will you give yours to Him?

"For the love of Christ controls us, because we are convinced that one has died for all; therefore all have died. And he died for all, that those who live might live no longer for themselves but for him who for their sake has died and was raised" (2 Cor. 5:14-15).

1. Why did Jesus die and why was He raised from the dead?
2. Because the sinful part of each one of us died with Jesus on the cross, what can now control our lives?
3. Because of Jesus' sacrifice, what should be the purpose of your life?

Why Don't We Go to Church on Tuesday?

Traditions are not easily changed. Even teenagers tell substitute teachers that it's "wrong" to have to write out answers to questions at the end of the chapter because the "real teacher" always has class discussions. Can you imagine eating tunafish sandwiches for Christmas dinner or having our Congress adopt a flag that's orange and purple? Would you object to having school begin at 6:00 a.m. or having the boys' basketball team wear kilts? People just don't change familiar ways unless they have a good reason for doing so.

Now, the Jewish people had a very strong tradition supported by one of the Ten Commandments, " 'Remember the sabbath day, to keep it holy.' " They observed a special day of rest and worship each Saturday because when God created the world He rested on the seventh day.

Only something very drastic would cause Jewish people to change their day of worship. But the most important event of history, the Resurrection, occurred on the first day of the week. Ignatius, the Bishop of Antioch, wrote in A.D. 110, "If, then, those who walk in the ancient practice attain to newness of hope, no longer observing the Sabbath but fashioning their lives after the Lord's Day on which our life also arose through Him, that we may be found disciples of Jesus Christ, our only teacher."[2]

Jesus' death and resurrection is so important that everything changes. The person who accepts Jesus is transformed from the inside out. Paul writes, "He who loves his neighbor has fulfilled the law" (Rom. 13:8). Paul writes that, because Jesus died and rose, "therefore let no one pass judgment on you in questions of food and drink or with regard to a festival or a new moon or a sabbath. These are only a shadow of what is to come; but the substance belongs to Christ" (Col. 2:16-17).

The Jews observed the Sabbath because the law required it. But Christians made Sunday their Sabbath because they wanted to celebrate their resurrection life.

The fact that Christians worship on Sunday is one of the great historical proofs that Jesus rose from the dead. The twelve apostles—all Jewish—wouldn't have started having services on Sunday just for the fun of it. And we won't begin Thursday schools or Tuesday morning worship services because nothing as great as the resurrection of Jesus will ever again take place in history.

Our Sunday worship should be more than a remembrance of the resurrection. It should remind us that the Jesus who walked on the water, healed the blind, and conquered death is capable of repeat performances.

"When the disciples reached the other side, they had forgotten to bring any bread. Jesus said to them, 'Take heed and beware of the leaven of the Pharisees and Sadducees.' And they discussed it among themselves, saying, 'We brought no bread.' But Jesus, aware of this, said, 'O men of little faith, why do you discuss among yourselves the fact that you have no bread? Do you not yet perceive? Do you not remember the five loaves of the five thousand, and how many baskets you gathered? Or the seven loaves of the four thousand, and how many baskets you gathered?' " (Matt. 16:5-10).

1. List the miracles of Jesus you remember from the Bible. Now list the times He miraculously helped you through tough situations.
2. Why is it easy for you, like the disciples, to worry about the little things, when Jesus has helped you through much harder situations?
3. What circumstance in your life, like the bread the disciples had forgotten to bring, is causing you concern? Read your list of the miracles of Jesus and get God's perspective on the situation.

No Zits in Heaven!

The resurrection of Jesus has something to say to you each morning as you look into the mirror and face all those pimples, those glasses as thick as Coke-bottle bottoms or that skinny bod. Well, just hang on a minute and you might learn something.

Jesus died a physical death and His risen body was real. Before Jesus died, He said, " 'Father, into thy hands I commit my spirit!' " (Luke 23:46). Then He "breathed his last." The Bible teaches that death is a separation of the body from the spirit, as explained in Ecclesiastes 12:7: "The dust returns to the earth as it was, and

the spirit returns to God who gave it." Jesus' spirit therefore left His body at death.

However, when Peter describes Jesus as "being put to death in the flesh but made alive in the spirit" (1 Pet. 3:18), it does not mean that the resurrection of Jesus was only spiritual and that His body evaporated into gases or was "invaded by Satan," because three verses later we find these words: "through the resurrection of Jesus Christ, who [not 'whose spirit'] has gone into heaven and is at the right hand of God." Romans 8:11 teaches us that God raised Jesus in *physical* form *through* the Holy Spirit: "If the Spirit of him who raised Jesus from the dead dwells in you, he who raised Christ Jesus from the dead will give life to your mortal bodies also THROUGH his Spirit which dwells in you." Scripture also tells us that the body of Jesus did not rot in the grave: " 'He whom God raised up saw no corruption' " (Acts 13:37).

On that first Easter, Jesus' spirit returned to the same body and brought it to life. The position of the grave clothes demonstrated this so clearly that Peter and John took one look and believed.

That the risen Jesus had a physical body is clearly demonstrated. Matthew 28:9 tells us, "And behold, Jesus met them and said, 'Hail!' And they came up and took hold of his *feet* and worshiped him." Jesus said to Thomas, " 'Put your finger here, and see my *hands*; and put out your hand, and place it in my *side*; do not be faithless, but believing' " (John 20:27). This resurrection body of Jesus could *eat* a piece of broiled fish (Luke 24:42), yet could go through walls (John 20:19) and ascend into heaven (Acts 1:9)!

The Bible teaches that because Jesus rose from the dead, our mortal bodies will also be resurrected. Jesus promised: " 'The hour is coming when all who are in the tombs will hear his voice and come forth, those who have done good, to the resurrection of life, and those who have done evil, to the resurrection of judgment' " (John 5:28-29). If you have given your life completely to Jesus, you'll be very interested in this " 'resurrection of life.' " Paul writes, "We await a Savior, the Lord Jesus Christ, who will *change our lowly body to be like his glorious body*" (Phil. 3:20-21). Some day you'll have a glorious body just like Jesus. There won't be any zits in heaven!

"Lo! I tell you a mystery. We shall not all sleep, but we shall all be changed, in a moment, in the twinkling of an eye, at the last trumpet. For the trumpet will sound, and the dead will be raised imperishable, and we shall be changed. For this perishable nature must put on the imperishable, and this mortal nature must put on immortality" (1 Cor. 15:51-53).

1. Why is it not sensible to worry endlessly about how you look and how to make yourself more presentable?
2. Next time that mirror discourages you, spend some time thanking God for the *new* body you're going to have in heaven.

Notes

Preface
1. Clark H. Pinnock, *Set Forth Your Case* (Chicago: Moody, 1971), p. 18.

Week One
1. *Biology* (Glenview, IL: Scott, Foresman, 1980), p. 12.
2. Francis A. Schaeffer, *The God Who Is There* (Downers Grove, IL: InterVarsity, 1971), p. 88.
3. J. I. Packer, *Knowing God* (Downers Grove, IL: Inter-Varsity, 1973), p. 42.
4. Paul E. Little, *Know Why You Believe* (Downers Grove, IL: Inter-Varsity, 1971), p. 54.
5. Louis Berkhof, *Manual of Christian Doctrine* (Grand Rapids: Eerdmans, 1965), p. 60.
6. Walter R. Martin, *The Kingdom of the Cults* (Minneapolis: Bethany House, 1977), p. 65.

Week Two
1. Rabi Maharaj, *Rebirth of a Yogi; Rabi Maharaj's Story* (Berkeley: Spiritual Counterfeits Project, no date), p. 6.
2. C. S. Lewis, *Mere Christianity* (New York: Macmillan, 1977), pp. 50-60.

Week Three
1. Lewis, *Mere Christianity,* p. 26.
2. *The Westminster Shorter Catechism* (1647), quoted in Philip Schaff, *The Creeds of Christendom,* 4th ed. rev. (Grand Rapids: Baker, 1966), p. 676.
3. William Law, *Wholly for God,* ed. Andrew Murray (Minneapolis: Bethany House, 1976), p. 228.

Week Four
1. Winkie Pratney, *The Holy Bible—Wholly True* (Lindale, TX: Pretty Good Printing, 1979).
2. Josh McDowell, *More Than a Carpenter* (Minneapolis: World Wide, 1977), p. 24.
3. Ibid., p. 31.
4. Harold Lindsell, *God's Incomparable Word* (Minneapolis: World Wide, 1977), p. 26.
5. Ibid., p. 26.
6. 2 Corinthians 6:14.
7. Lindsell, *God's Incomparable Word,* p. 22.
8. Ibid., p. 54.
9. Ibid., p. 71.
10. Ibid., p. 71.

11. Ephesians 6:1; Colosians 3:20.

12. Philippians 2:14.

13. Lindsell, *God's Incomparable Word*, p. 40.

14. Exodus 20:17.

Week Five

1. Little, *Know Why You Believe*, p. 73.

2. Ibid., p. 51.

3. Pinnock, *Set Forth Your Case*, p. 102.

4. Little, *Know Why You Believe*, p. 50.

5. lbid., p 50.

6. F. F. Bruce, *The New Testament Documents: Are They Reliable?* (Grand Rapids: Eerdmans, 1962), p. 21.

7. lbid., p. 27.

8. Little, *Know Why You Believe*, p. 47.

9. Bruce, *New Testament Documents*, p. 27.

10. J. N. Hawthorne, *Questions of Science and Faith* (London, 1960), p. 55, quoted in Little, *Know Why You Believe*, p. 62.

11. Bruce, *New Testament Documents*, p. 68.

12. Little, *Know Why You Believe*, pp. 64-65.

Week Six

1. *Encyclopaedia Britannica*, s.v. "Chronology."

2. Revelation 21:4.

3. John 3:16.

Week Seven

1. Bruce, *New Testament Documents*, p. 12.

2. Little, *Know Why You Believe*, p. 18.

3. lbid., p. 44.

4. Pinnock, *Set Forth Your Case*, p. 87.

5. John R.W. Stott, *Basic Christianity* (Downers Grove, IL: Inter-Varsity, 1972), p. 22.

6. Richard Wolff, *The Son of Man: Is Jesus Christ Unique?* (Lincoln, NB: Good News Broadcasting Association, 1960), p. 7.

7. lbid., p. 8.

8. lbid., pp. 8-9.

9. Jean-Jacques Rousseau, *Emile* (no pub. info.), IV, quoted in Wolff, *Son of Man*, p.17.

10. McDowell, *More Than a Carpenter*, p. 7.

11. Wolff, *Son of Man*, p. 50.

12. John 14:6.

13. John 8:12.

14. Lewis, *Mere Christianity* (New York: Macmillan, 1956), p. 41.

15. John 8:58, 45-46, 42-44.

16. Matthew 10:37.

17. C. S. Lewis, *Miracles: A Preliminary Study* (New York: Mac-

millan, 1947), p. 113. Quoted in Robert Crossley, *The Trinity* (See Week Ten, No. 2, below).

18. Wolff, *Son of Man,* pp. 49-50.

19. Luke 2:49.

20. Robert E. Hume, *The World's Living Religions* (New York: Scribner's, 1959), p. 65.

21. *Analects of Confucius,* 7:1, quoted in Ibid., p. 116.

22. Ibid., p. 61.

Week Eight

1. Stott, *Basic Christianity,* p. 27.

2. Matthew 5:44, 5:16, 6:25.

3. John 16:13.

4. 1 Timothy 1:15.

5. John 8:46.

6. John 1:3-4.

7. John 3:3, 5, 11; 5:19, 24, 25; 6:26, 32, 47; etc.

8. Matthew 6:34; 6:19.

Week Nine

1. Stott, *Basic Christianity,* p. 40.

2. Mark 14:62; Matthew 26:64.

3. Luke 23:41; Matthew 27:54.

4. Bruce Olson, *Bruchko* (Carol Stream, IL: Creation House, 1973).

5. McDowell, *More Than a Carpenter,* p. 8.

6. John 14:28; Luke 22:42; Mark 15:34.

7. John 20:28.

8. Stott, *Basic Christianity,* p. 24.

Week Ten

1. Martin, *Kingdom of the Cults,* p. 61.

2. Robert Crossley, *The Trinity* (Downers Grove, IL: InterVarsity, 1977), p. 18.

3. C. S. Lewis, *The Problem of Pain* (Huntington, NY, n.d.), p. 29, cited in Crossley, *Trinity,* p. 41.

Week Eleven

1. McDowell, *More Than a Carpenter,* p. 60.

2. F. Davidson, A. M. Stibbs, and E. F. Kevan, eds., *The New Bible Commentary* (Grand Rapids: Eerdmans, 1960), p. 828.

3. *Encyclopaedia Britannica,* s.v. "Crucifixion."

4. Schaeffer, *The God Who Is There,* p. 128.

5. McDowell, *More Than a Carpenter,* p. 61. (The other verses are Psalm 118:26, Daniel 9:26, Zechariah 11:13 and Haggai 2:7-9.)

6. Ibid., pp. 61-62.

Week Twelve

1. *Encyclopaedia Britannica,* s.v. "Easter."

2. Henry H. Halley, *Halley's Bible Handbook,* 24th ed. (Grand Rapids: Zondervan, 1965), p. 453.

3. *Christ's Last Week* (Minneapolis: Holy Land Bible Knowledge Society, n.d.).

4. Josh McDowell, *Evidence That Demands a Verdict* (San Bernadino, CA: Campus Crusade for Christ, 1972), p. 85.

5. Stott, *Basic Christianity,* pp. 53-54.

Week Thirteen

1. Acts 20:35.

2. Martin, *Kingdom of the Cults,* p. 395.

For Further Study

Bruce, F. F. *The New Testament Documents: Are They Reliable?* Grand Rapids: Eerdmans, 1962.

Crossley, Robert. *The Trinity.* Downers Grove, IL: InterVarsity, 1977.

Halley, Henry H. *Halley's Bible Handbook.* 24th ed. Grand Rapids: Zondervan, 1965.

Hume, Robert E. *The World's Living Religions.* New York: Scribner's, 1959.

Law, William. *Wholly for God.* Edited by Andrew Murray. Minneapolis: Bethany House, 1976.

Lewis, C. S. *Mere Christianity.* New York: Macmillan, 1977.

Lindsell, Harold. *God's Incomparable Word.* Minneapolis: World Wide, 1977.

Little, Paul E. *Know Why You Believe.* Downers Grove IL: InterVarsity, 1971.

Martin, Walter R. *The Kingdom of the Cults.* Minneapolis: Bethany House, 1977.

McDowell, Josh. *Evidence That Demands a Verdict.* San Bernadino, CA: Campus Crusade for Christ, 1972.

McDowell, Josh. *More Than a Carpenter.* Minneapolis: World Wide, 1977.

Olson, Bruce. *Bruchko.* Carol Stream, IL: Creation House, 1973.

Parker, J. I. *Knowing God.* Downers Grove, IL: InterVarsity, 1973.

Pinnock, Clark H. *Set Forth Your Case.* Chicago: Moody, 1971.

Schaeffer, Francis A. *The God Who Is There.* Downers Grove, IL: InterVarsity, 1971.

Stott, John R.W. *Basic Christianity.* Downers Grove, IL: InterVarsity, 1972.

Wolff, Richard. *Son of Man: Is Jesus Christ Unique?* Lincoln. NB: Good News Broadcasting Association, 1960.